SIX DISCIPLINES®
EXECUTION
REVOLUTION

Thanks to the Following Pioneers Who Helped Prove the Concepts in *Six Disciplines® Execution Revolution*

"GreaterFindlayInc." (GFI) is a hybrid Chamber of Commerce and economic development organization, providing the area's best development and business advocacy resources to the Greater Findlay (Ohio) region.

The program described in *Execution Revolution* has positioned GFI to run a more efficient, accountable and focused organization in a way that better serves our members and our community. This complete strategy execution program provides my staff and me a clear roadmap to moving both the organization and the interests of the Greater Findlay area forward."

> — Douglas Peters, IOM, CCEO-AP
> President & CEO, GreaterFindlayInc.

■　■　■

A to Z Portion Control Meats, Inc. produces Federally Inspected Beef, Pork and Chicken items for full line food distributors. A to Z Meats has over a fifty year history as a family owned and operated processing plant. Running a family business presents unique challenges. I've experienced first-hand the devastation to family relationships that I now know were the result of poor communication, lack of clear expectations and accountability.

The program described in *Execution Revolution* has given us the tools for implementing and working toward sustaining success and moving toward excellence. Reading *Execution Revolution* reaffirmed my enthusiasm for practicing the complete strategy execution program as the vehicle that will bring this fifty-plus year old family business into a culture of accountability, strategy and strength."

> — LEE ANN KAGY
> President & CEO, A to Z Portion Control Meats, Inc.

■ ■ ■

World Class Plastics, Inc. is a provider of custom, thermoplastic, injection molded product. Since its start in 1994, WCPI has grown to be a two-state, just-in-time manufacturing operation. Our efforts towards truly being 'World Class' have often illustrated the impact that true focus and execution have on an organization and the struggle that exists to maintain those abilities.

The complete strategy execution program outlined in *Execution Revolution* is the system that is now aiding us in our continuous effort to be World Class.

> — MARK SEELEY
> President, World Class Plastics, Inc.

■ ■ ■

Total Fleet Solutions (TFS) was founded in 1999. Asset management of technology assets was a trend in the 1990's and TFS was able to create a market by applying that concept to the material handling industry. Today TFS is a multi-national company that manages over 15,000 material handling assets from inception through disposal. Our growth is a result of executing our strategy by continuing to innovate while maintaining a high level of customer satisfaction.

The complete strategy execution program detailed in *Execution Revolution* has helped improve the alignment of our management team's daily activities to the company's strategic initiatives. This improved process will create additional value for our customers and shareholders because we now know that everything we work on is in alignment with where the company needs to be and where it is going.

— Todd W. Roberts
CEO, Total Fleet Solutions

▪ ▪ ▪

Trufast LLC, founded in 1981, is a fastener manufacturer serving the commercial and residential construction industry. Since the year 2000, Trufast has grown sales 15% annually. This rapid growth has brought many challenges to the organization.

We are practitioners of the program outlined in *Execution Revolution* to help management focus the organization on the opportunities that truly add value. Not only has it improved our strategic planning process, more importantly, *it provides the tools to allow us to execute the plan.* This is what separates the program outlined in *Execution Revolution* from all the other strategic planning processes I have been involved in.

— Brian Roth
President & CEO, Trufast, LLC

▪ ▪ ▪

Collman & Karsky Architects, Inc. of Tampa Florida offers +46 years of service and devotion to providing superior product and support for the fields of architecture, interior design, and client services. Satisfied clients are the key to our success.

For us, the *Execution Revolution* is underway! By following the principles in this book (and in *Six Disciplines for Excellence*) we have experienced a significant increase in billable time. As a result of this program, our teamwork and our ability to execute will continue to grow as we grow.

— Bryan Karsky
Executive Vice President,
Collman & Karsky Architects, Inc.

PRO-TEC Coating Company was established as a joint venture in 1990 by two global leaders in steel technology and production—U.S. Steel Corporation (USS) and Kobe Steel, Ltd., of Japan. It is one of the largest hot-dip galvanizing plant in North America, with a total production capability to over 1.1 million tons annually of high quality galvanized steel. Now with 236 employees, its 730,000-square-foot plant is located on a 1,200-acre site, near Leipsic, Ohio.

Numerous "best management" practices have been incorporated into PRO-TEC's corporate culture, including a self-directed workforce, lean manufacturing, continuous improvement, and an empowered workforce exercising ownership, responsibility, and accountability.

My initial reaction when I read *Execution Revolution* was that Gary Harpst has described the perfect compliment to *Six Disciplines for Excellence*. Execution focuses on the biggest challenge to any organization, which is, deployment of processes. The strategy execution program described in *Execution Revolution* has helped us accelerate our performance excellence journey.

> — PAUL WORSTELL
> President, PRO-TEC Coating Company
> (2007 Malcolm Baldrige National Quality Award Recipient)

Kellermeyer Company was founded in 1944 by Vernon Kellermeyer and his wife, Dorothy. Today, Kellermeyer is one of the largest distribution companies in the region specializing in janitorial supplies, industrial packaging products and industrial cleaning equipment. Kellermeyer employs over 70 team members and has branch offices in Ohio, Michigan and Indiana. The Kellermeyer main 100,000 sq. ft. distribution center is located in Bowling Green, Ohio.

Kellermeyer Company could be a poster child for what Gary Harpst has described in *Execution Revolution*. We tried it all in the past: consultants, computer programs, internal planning and more—but nothing "stuck." Strategic planning became a joke in the organization, and the employees saw no value and had no input as to where the company wanted to go. I knew when I was named President, there had to be a better way. When I discovered Six Disciplines, I found what I was looking for. The repeatable methodology described in *Execution Revolution* works. All employees now know where our company is going and how they personally help achieve company goals. It has also strengthened our communication, management skills, and most importantly, our results.

— JILL KEGLER
President, Kellermeyer Company

Additional Advance Praise for
Six Disciplines® Execution Revolution

"Harpst has put together a map for building enduring excellence into your business—with clear instructions for how to get from 'here' to 'there.' You won't find it spelled out any better than this!"

> — DAN BOBINSKI, CEO/Director,
> The Center for Workplace Excellence

"Harpst has created an upbeat and easy-to-follow roadmap for any one who is a part of a business that must grow and succeed. The lessons in *Execution Revolution* are not only direct and straightforward, but also provide hope and inspiration for the "little guys" who do not have the resources of a Fortune 100 company. Get ready for a healthy dose of clarity for what's ailing your organization and what you can do about it, starting today."

> — MARK WISKUP, International Business
> Communication Skills Consultant and
> author of *The IT Factor* and *Presentation S.O.S.*

"*Execution Revolution* tackles a very complex subject in a very realistic and practical way. It strikes a nice balance between the complexities of knowing 'what to do' with a practical approach to the less than exciting task of 'doing it'. Nice job!"

> — STEVE MACGILL, Founder, PeerSight

"*Execution Revolution* answers WHY the right balance of strategy and execution achieves enduring excellence, and most importantly, HOW to achieve it. Read this book TODAY!"

> — ZANE SAFRIT, CEO, Conference Calls Unlimited

"Don't be left behind! Join the Execution Revolution and see what your business truly is capable of achieving."

> — SKIP ANGEL, Consultant, Solutions IQ

SIX DISCIPLINES®
EXECUTION
REVOLUTION

Solving the One Business Problem That Makes
Solving All Other Problems *Easier*

GARY HARPST

AUTHOR OF *SIX DISCIPLINES FOR EXCELLENCE*

SIX DISCIPLINES
PUBLISHING

Six Disciplines® Execution Revolution:
Solving the One Business Problem
That Makes Solving All Other Problems Easier

Published by Six Disciplines Publishing
Findlay, Ohio 45840
www.SixDisciplinesPublishing.com

Six Disciplines and Be Excellent are
registered trademarks of Six Disciplines, LLC.

The four-quadrant Business Excellence Model
is a trademark of Six Disciplines, LLC.

ISBN-13: 978-0-9816411-0-2

Copyright © 2008 by Gary Harpst

Book Cover: Greenleaf Book Group, LLC
Interior Design: Desktop Miracles, Inc.

Printed in the United States of America

Publisher's Cataloging-In-Publication Data
(Prepared by The Donohue Group, Inc.)

Harpst, Gary.
    Six disciplines execution revolution : solving the one business
problem that makes solving all other problems easier / Gary
Harpst.
        p. : ill., charts ; cm.
    Includes bibliographical references and index.
    ISBN–13: 978–0–9816411–0–2
    ISBN–10: 0–9816411–0–5
    1. Organizational effectiveness.   2. Strategic planning.
3. Performance.   4. Success in business.   I. Title.
HD58.9 .H3777   2008
                                                                658.4/01

Contents

Introduction

All revolutions are based on a core set of ideas. The ideas in this book emerged from my twenty-seven years of experience as CEO and co-founder of three businesses. Twenty of those years were with Solomon Software, which implemented more than 60,000 business management systems in small and midsized businesses, across almost every industry imaginable, before it was eventually sold to Microsoft.[1]

Since that time, I've focused my attention on helping other businesses benefit from the many mistakes I made as a CEO, and the mistakes I see others make every day. This book describes the cumulative learning after investing $20 million, and over 100 man-years of research and field experience.

The first premise of this book is that what most business leaders think is their greatest challenge really *isn't*. All business leaders face new challenges each day and are tempted to think of the latest problem at hand as their "biggest." No matter what the problems are today, however, they'll be different tomorrow and they will be bigger. This leads to the next premise of this book.

There is one business problem that, if solved, makes solving all other problems *easier*. Knowing how to plan and execute, while overcoming "today's surprises," is the most foundational capability any organization can have. The inability to do this is the problem that business leaders must solve. With the capability to execute continuously, they gain control of their businesses. Without it, their businesses are relegated to a reactive, firefighting existence.

The final premise of this book is that an opportunity exists for small and midsized businesses to leapfrog a whole generation of impractical, large-company approaches that have been used to attack this problem. Over the past few decades, progress in a variety of best practices and technologies (primarily funded by large businesses) has created the foundation for a next-generation program that will overcome the barriers keeping solutions out of reach for all but the largest of businesses.

Most business leaders I know started their business journey with visions of excellence in their head and heart but frequently get so absorbed by the day-to-day challenges of their business that they never really figure out what excellence means for them. I know—I'm one of them. In most of my twenty-year tenure as CEO of Solomon Software, I was in react mode, moving from one crisis to the next. By most people's standards, our business was very successful since it grew from a startup to $60 million in revenue in twenty years. I now realize, however, that if I had focused on solving the one problem that is the subject of this book, we would've grown to multiples of that size—and, with fewer headaches.

In this book, I'm suggesting that excellence is the enduring pursuit of balanced strategy *and* execution. Strategy requires choosing what promises to make to all stakeholders and a roadmap for delivering on those promises. Execution requires getting there, while overcoming unending surprises.

Of the two, execution is far more difficult to achieve, but is fruitless without solid strategy. Learning how to balance these two is the key to excellence. Excellence is a journey that never ends. It's an enduring pursuit that requires an enduring approach.

Somehow on this journey we often lose sight of what the real problem is. As already stated, it's *not* what most business leaders think. Most describe their biggest challenge as the issue(s) they're facing right now (growth, control, communication, productivity, generational transition, hiring, competitors, and many others.) Whatever issues an organization faces today, they will be different and bigger tomorrow. Planning and executing, while at the *same time*, managing the unknowns of the real world, is the biggest challenge in business. Overcoming this challenge is what we mean by solving the problem that will make solving all other problems easier. It builds an organization that is preparing for an ever increasing set of *future* challenges that are the natural result of overcoming *today's* challenges.

Given the pace and unpredictability of the business world, we leaders often feel there's not much that we do control. This book, however, describes the first *complete* program for a business to take control of the one thing it can, so that it is better equipped to deal with all the things it can't. It's my hope that the real-world experience of our team, the investment that's been made, and the completeness of the program will help you realize this isn't just another book. It's the beginning of a revolution—an *Execution Revolution*.

CHAPTER 1

[Business Excellence]

" After many years, I've finally come to view excellence as the enduring pursuit of balanced strategy and execution. "

Before tackling the biggest problem in business, we need to drop back to a more foundational topic. We need to define strategy, execution, and their relationship to business excellence.

In my experience, most leaders of small and midsized organizations do not have a clear understanding of the relationship between strategy, execution, and excellence. This is easy for me to believe because, as a CEO of a successful company for twenty years, I didn't understand these principles myself. Most business leaders are so consumed by their businesses they don't take the time to develop such perspectives.

The purpose of this chapter is to weave strategy and execution into a single model for understanding enduring business excellence. We'll provide a common framework for a meaningful dialogue about where you are in terms of your business, how you got there, and how to develop a vision of where you'd like to go.

What Is Excellence?

Whenever I meet business leaders, I take the opportunity to ask them two questions: (1) What does excellence mean to you? and (2) Do you think you've achieved it? Two truths emerge. First, no two people define excellence exactly the same way. Their definition evolves as they learn and as circumstances change. Second, nearly everyone agrees that excellence is a journey, not a destination. As a result, no one who's serious about excellence believes he or she is "there" yet.

The conclusion is that excellence is an enduring pursuit and, therefore, requires an enduring approach. According to Samuel Johnson, excellence is a "lifelong pursuit for most who attain it. Nothing less will do."

After many years, I've finally come to see that excellence requires on-going balance between strategy and execution. Strategy requires choosing what promises to make to all stakeholders and a roadmap for delivering on those promises. Execution requires *getting there* while overcoming an unending number of surprises. Of the two, execution is far more difficult to achieve, but it is impossible without solid strategy. Learning how to continually balance these two is the key to excellence. This is why excellence is a journey that never ends. Everyone, however, doesn't see it that way. To illustrate, let me relate one story. I was speaking to a large Chamber of Commerce recently, and, after I posed these two questions ("what is excellence?" and "have you achieved it?") to the assembly, one woman said she thought she had achieved excellence. This response was highly unusual.

I tried not to show surprise during my speech, but quickly made a note to myself to speak to her after the event. When I finally did talk to "Jan," I asked what business she was in and how she had turned it into an *excellent one.* Her answer was not what I expected.

I learned that she ran a fairly small business that provided portable storage units, and she was ecstatic because sales had almost doubled in the last thirty days. I asked if she knew why, but she didn't.

It turned out this spike in sales occurred three weeks after a flood in the area. So I probed a little to find out whether she thought this unfortunate situation might have driven demand temporarily. She didn't believe this was the reason, thinking her good fortune was a mark of excellence.

I walked away wondering about her notion of excellence, and whether she'd think her organization was excellent in twelve months. I recognized this short-term mindset only because I'd been where she was many times in my life as an entrepreneur and business owner—before I began to see this pattern in my own thinking.

Introducing the Business Excellence Model

Simply put, the focus and capability of an organization can be understood in two dimensions: strategy (deciding what to do) and execution (getting it done). Figure 1.0 shows a model of these dimensions using four quadrants of performance. Quadrant I is strong strategy with weak execution, Quadrant II is strong strategy with strong execution, and so forth.

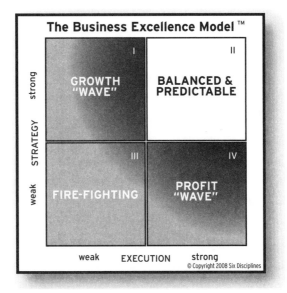

Figure 1.0–The Business Excellence Model

Leaders who build organizations with the ability to balance strong strategy with strong execution over long periods of time achieve *enduring excellence*. In this chapter, we'll explore the topic of excellence more completely. And, in the remainder of the book, we'll explore how you can go about pursuing it.

Before moving on, I want to acknowledge Michael Porter for his profound and comprehensive views on strategy. In particular, I recommend his well-known article, "What is Strategy?" which is available from *Harvard Business Review*.[1]

In the article, Porter summarizes strategy as choosing a set of activities, a *different* and *unique* set of activities that sets one apart from the competition. Porter summarizes, "the essence of strategy is choosing what *not* to do." In other words, creating a distinctive strategy is all about making good choices, as well as good trade-offs. Southwest Airlines illustrated the power of such choice years ago when it set out to specialize in short, direct-connect flights and chose *not* to be a global airline.

Now, let's consider the execution dimension (horizontal axis) of the business excellence model. This dimension is character-ized by a relentless drive for improvement: seeking to perform a chosen set of activities *better* than the competition. While strategy is about combining best choices and similar activities, execution is all about continual improvement in those chosen activities.

This combination of strategy (the choices of what to do versus what not to do) and execution (how well the choices are carried out) becomes the field upon which the Execution Revolution occurs in any given company.

How well an organization performs both strategy and execu-tion determines its capability and capacity to sustain business excellence over time. Most organizations cycle through all four quadrants in this model—and do so repeatedly. The world we live in is too unpredictable for this not to be true. The adoption of a strategy execution program, as discussed in Chapter 6, however, helps an organization maximize the time spent in Quadrant II.

Let's look more closely at how businesses operate and focus their activities while they are in each of the four quadrants of business excellence.

Quadrant I: Strong Strategy/Weak Execution

We begin our exploration of the business excellence model in Quadrant I (Figure 1.1). In this quadrant, a business has a strong strategy, which typically means a competitive advantage. This advantage can come from offering premium products or services, availability, or price. It can be rooted in technology, distribution channels, manufacturing expertise, or current customer base. Some start-ups enter the market with a "better mousetrap" than those of long-standing companies.

Regardless of whether a company is a start-up or a seasoned business, strong strategy usually leads to a growth in sales. This kind of company has something people want, with some advantage over the competition. Maybe this advantage is easy to copy or maybe it's not. But one thing is certain: if it works, the competition will follow.

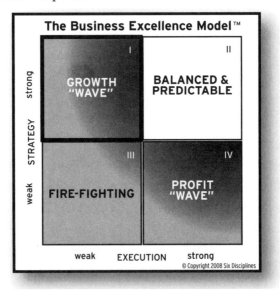

Figure 1.1–Quadrant I: Strong strategy/weak execution

A good illustration of a Quadrant I situation is Sharn Veterinary of Tampa, Florida, in its very early days of operation.[2] Sharn founder Andy Schultz, a retiree from a medical supply company, had noticed over the years that there was a demand for human-quality medical monitoring equipment, such as blood pressure devices, to serve the veterinary market.

In 2001, Sharn was a perfect example of the start-up that begins in Quadrant I with a big competitive advantage and a long-term focus on an underserved niche market. The result was that Sharn quickly became the leader in that market. In fact, Schultz's business grew to the point where he could no longer handle it by himself and began adding people. This is exactly what happens in Quadrant I—a tremendous increase in sales, leading to growth throughout the organization.

Other successful start-up companies, whose stories are now familiar, and who also began with a strong strategy, include Red Bull (energy drink), Netflix (movie rentals), Dell (computers direct), and Google (internet search). For these companies, the basis of success in Quadrant I was making clear choices about what they would and would not provide to customers. And their choices reflected what they believed would provide a competitive advantage. The resulting success has proven that their choices were good ones.

Now consider a few runaway successes from several *established market leaders*. Apple's iPod (portable entertainment) or iPhone (internet-driven phone) and Nintendo's Wii (active participation video games) are examples of how new products and services from existing organizations can drive growth.

In fact, these runaway successes are growing so rapidly that it's putting pressure on the ability of those companies to execute—to deliver enough quality product to meet demand. This is a key point to understand. Success and the results of growth start the journey—but this often leads an organization (and its leadership) into Quadrant IV.

Quadrant IV: Strong Execution/Weak Strategy

Before we discuss the details of Quadrant IV (Figure 1.2), this is a good point to emphasize that the business excellence model offered here is a simple one, designed to promote understanding in a very complex business world. Because of its simplicity, it's also easy to come up with scenarios this model does not explain. But we've found this tool to be very useful in helping companies understand what's happening to them and why.

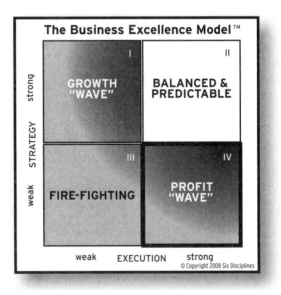

Figure 1.2–Quadrant IV: Strong execution/weak strategy

In the real world, there's no clear line between these quadrants. Also, businesses don't usually stay in one quadrant, as illustrated in Figure 1.3, where the focus of the organization and its priorities gradually change, and the company drifts between quadrants.

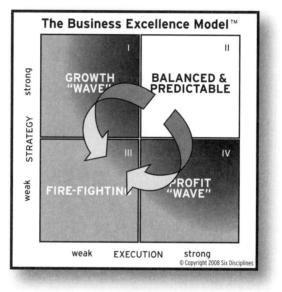

Figure 1.3–Drifting between quadrants in the business excellence model

Let's continue with the Sharn Veterinary example. For some time, Sharn devoted its time and energy (focus) to creating—a breakthrough product. The company wasn't as focused on supporting this product as it was creating it and getting it established. Once established, Sharn's focus rightfully changed to meeting the demand for the product, servicing it, and eventually harvesting increasing profits from it.

Especially for smaller organizations, as each of these phases occur, it's very difficult to maintain focus on thinking about and building the next growth driver while everyone's clamoring for more of the current offering.

Therefore, a company in Quadrant IV usually gets there because it's experiencing the pains of growth. Quite often, sales have outpaced capacity, so leadership becomes *focused* on strengthening internal operations, to address quality, scheduling, hiring, training, customer service, order processing, and other issues. In other words, the movement into Quadrant IV is a natural reaction to success in Quadrant I.

If an organization can manage the current growth wave efficiently *and* at the same time continues to invest effectively on the next growth wave, then it enters Quadrant II, characterized by balanced growth and profitability and more predictable business.

This isn't the case for most companies, where growing pains push them into Quadrant IV instead of Quadrant II. Problems such as customer complaints and inadequate supply redirect the focus of the leadership team to operation and execution issues.

Here lies the challenge of staying in Quadrant II (I speak from experience). Strong strategy and strong execution are *individually* so demanding that the earlier stages of each often require more than 100 percent of leadership and management's attention. There were times when Solomon Software sustained a 30- to 50-percent growth rate for several years in a row, and it was all we could do to service our clients. Since operational issues were more urgent, they got the attention of leadership.

Interestingly, this singular focus usually causes another problem to sneak up unannounced: the loss of the original competitive advantage, gained while operating in Quadrant I. Sometimes the focus on execution becomes so intense that a company doesn't make the investments required to protect and sustain its strategy advantages. Sales slow down, profits decline, and the company turns its focus to such issues as efficiency and cost savings. If this focus is pursued too hard and a company remains in this rut too long, it will slip into the weak state of Quadrant III, where it has neither strong growth nor good profitability.

Quadrant III: Weak Strategy/Weak Execution

It's easy for a company to flounder in Quadrant III for quite a while before leadership really accepts that they are there. At first, declining growth rates are excused as an aberration or some short-term cause. The shift into this state of weakness results from a gradual decline in growth and profitability, caused by decisions made (or not made) a year or two earlier. With slowing sales growth management is often pressured to increase profitability through efficiency gains that may cut muscle and not fat. This makes the company weaker, confidence declines, and even the little problems become big ones. In my experience, a company in Quadrant III is very reactive and frequently in chaos, operating daily in firefighting mode without a clear path out of their circumstances.

I recall coaching a small IT organization whose founder/CEO operated the company by doing nearly everything himself. This man worked more than eighty hours per week, seven days a week. In a planning meeting I conducted with his leadership team, it became evident how overwhelmed he was from these activities.

It was also evident that he was unwilling to delegate anything. All the ideas for improving the business were added to

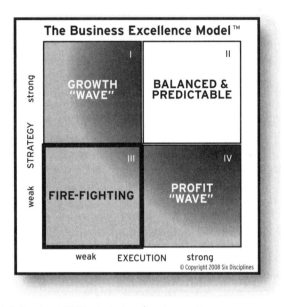

Figure 1.4–Quadrant III: Weak strategy/weak execution

his plate, and yet he wouldn't drop anything. Ultimately we couldn't help this client because its CEO was unwilling to make the tough decisions necessary to get out of Quadrant III. It was obvious to his leaders what was going on, and they were preparing to leave the organization because of his inability to change.

This is how Quadrant III (Figure 1.4) businesses operate. Overworked, confused and eventually a feeling of hopelessness if not addressed. Interestingly, by the time we recognize we're in Quadrant III, we're probably at least two years away from fixing the problem. Why? Because we have to start the growth cycle all over again and that usually takes significant time.

Clearly, having an organization operate in this quadrant is *not* where a CEO wants his company to be for any length of time. Unfortunately, some business leaders never figure out how to escape it and the company becomes what one of my former board members, David Johnston, calls the "living dead."

The picture does *not* have to be so grim. Business leaders who recognize what has happened *can* learn to change the behaviors that got them into this undesirable growth-profitability cycle in the first place. I doubt any organization or leadership team is so good that it will never spend any time in Quadrant III. But I do believe that leaders can minimize the time spent here if they're proactive in learning how to balance execution with strategy.

Typically, the best exit plan for moving out of Quadrant III is to aggressively reallocate resources from low-profitability areas to the growth areas. This sounds easy, but most organizations don't have the framework, the will, or the persistence to make the hard choices it requires.

Quadrant II: Strong Strategy/Strong Execution

Quadrant II (Figure 1.5) is all about balancing growth with profitability and performing predictably. This requires a disciplined organization, one that's able to execute well enough to address the needs of today and build for tomorrow at the same time. Poor execution and poor operations usually drain so much resource and leadership attention that preparations for future growth are sacrificed.

Sustainable excellence isn't possible unless an organization learns to systematically increase its capability to execute, and to do so *faster* than the rate at which its challenges are growing. It's ironic that the better an organization executes today, the bigger its challenges will be tomorrow. This is why it's so difficult to

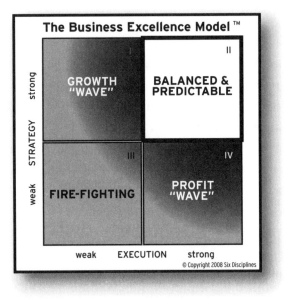

Figure 1.5–Quadrant II–Strong strategy/strong execution

balance strategy and execution over the long-term. Without an aggressive, proactive approach, organizations cannot identify or address their challenges in sufficient time, to avoid drifting into another quadrant. Remember that growth or efficiency issues can take years to address. The sooner they are caught and addressed, the lower variability (risk) a business undergoes.

Volumes have been written about Wal-Mart's obsession with efficiency. Considering that this retailing giant employs more than 1.9 million associates in 6,500 stores worldwide, its consistent ability to execute on its "everyday low price" strategy is astounding.

Clearly, Wal-Mart has embraced a culture of constant measurement and monitoring, where the mantra is "better, faster, cheaper." Few can argue with its overwhelming success. Some leaders tend to dismiss the Wal-Mart example because it's so big. That wasn't always the case. Wal-Mart began in 1962 as a single store in Arkansas, owned by a guy driving a pickup truck. They are not great at execution because they're big, they're big because they're great at executing their strategy.

What makes Wal-Mart an amazing example of a Quadrant II company is its ability to continually balance growth and profitability. Wal-Mart's international sales volume has attained a 27.4 percent compound annual growth rate over the past seven years. Sam Walton began with $72,000 in annual revenue, grew this at 29 percent per year for three decades, and then accelerated from there. In recent years, the company has settled into 16 percent per year average growth—but from a much larger base. That kind of cumulative growth achieved over seven decades turns a $72,000 dime store into a $1 trillion corporation!

There are a number of other big-name companies that have been successful at maintaining balanced growth and earnings for long period of times—General Electric, Microsoft, McDonalds, and Toyota, to name just a few.

Admittedly, Quadrant II performance is difficult to sustain. Few companies are able to achieve this kind of performance for long periods of time. But this is what the Execution Revolution is all about: the process of changing the game with regard to enduring business excellence by focusing on how to plan and execute strategy more effectively while successfully managing the surprises along the way.

Where Are You Now?

The business excellence model we're describing is not about company size. Every successful company once started small.

This model, however, is very useful in helping leaders of businesses of *any* size understand where they are now. It offers insight into some of the forces that got them there, and it helps the organization anticipate what could happen next. When we put this business excellence model in front of business leaders, they quickly point to where they think their company is today.

We've had clients use this model and label their businesses as being good or bad based on which quadrant they're in. That's not the purpose. Rather, we encourage business leaders instead to think of the business excellence model as a map that provides guidance about where to go next. *Any* company that's been around for awhile has traveled through *all* of these quadrants. The ultimate objective is to grow the capability of your organization to stay in Quadrant II for longer and longer periods of time.

[SUMMARY]

- No two people define excellence in exactly the same way, and nearly everyone agrees that excellence is a journey—not a destination.
- A business excellence model can be used that plots how organizations operate relative to the two dimensions of strategy and execution.
- Organizations in Quadrant I exhibit strong strategy, which typically translates into a competitive advantage. They are characterized by periods or waves of growth and market share gains.
- Organizations in Quadrant IV exhibit strong operational execution, focused on doing things "better, faster, cheaper." They are characterized by periods or waves of profitability.

- Organizations in Quadrant III are typically weak in both strategy and execution, and frequently find themselves firefighting with daily issues.
- Organizations in Quadrant II exhibit an appropriate balance between strategy and execution, and are characterized by predictable growth.
- Quadrant II performance is difficult to sustain. Very few companies are able to achieve this kind of performance for long periods of time, but the time is right for a new way to approach strategy and execution in order to do so.

Today, we're on the cusp of a radical shift—a next-generation approach for how organizations are able to pursue the endless journey of business excellence. This journey starts with the realization by leadership that the particular challenge of the moment is merely a symptom of a deeper need of all growing organizations: the need to systematically improve the organization's ability to manage the *next* challenge.

Using the business excellence model, we're now ready to drill down on the types of problems that businesses face and the *one* that is the "biggest" problem of all. Chapter 2 is the key to grasping why solving this problem makes solving all other problems *easier.* Read on!

[The Biggest Problem in Business]

> **"** Concentrate on solving the
> problem that makes all the
> other problems soluble. **"**
>
> —*Holman W. Jenkins, Jr.,*
> *Wall Street Journal*

The Introduction to this book listed three core premises, two of which are repeated here. First, what most business leaders think their greatest challenge is, *isn't*. And whatever their problems are today, they'll be different tomorrow and they will be bigger too. Second, there is one business problem that if solved, will make solving all other problems easier. This foundational challenge is executing strategy. In other words, building an organization that has the ability to plan and execute, while at the same time, overcoming the inevitable surprises in business. *This is the biggest and toughest challenge in business.*

This chapter explores the variety of challenges that businesses face every single day. More importantly, we're going to examine premise 2: the one problem, that if it is solved, will make doing business easier. Notice I didn't say easy—just *easier.*

In thirty years of working with small and midsized businesses, I've asked thousands of business leaders to name their biggest challenges. The answers vary widely, from competitive issues, cash flow, finding the right people, and communication to sales, marketing, technology, and lack of engagement.

A fundamental idea of this book is that none of these "current" issues are the real challenge. Building an organization that executes is the greatest competence an organization can have and doing so is the greatest challenge. Using a nautical analogy, every business can be thought of as a ship. Most ships takes on some water through a leak here and there, or through unexpected waves that come over the side. Any ship that is going to get anywhere must have a crew who can bail water out as it comes on, and be able to man the engines, navigate, and so on, to arrive at the destination on time. Progressing to the destination on time all the while bailing water is what we call strategy execution. Doing these things on every voyage is what we call excellence.

Building an organization that can plan, execute and address surprises is not easy. The alternative, however, is that every time "water" comes on board, you put all hands on deck to bail—and the ship drifts. This is exactly what happens to every business that finds itself operating in Quadrant III.

In this chapter, I want you to think differently about what your biggest challenge really is, or as Holman Jenkins so aptly put it, to focus "on solving the problem that makes all the other problems soluble."

What Business Leaders SAY Are Their Greatest Challenges

Perhaps you've heard the old adage that defining the problem is 80 percent of the solution? To dig a little deeper on how most business leaders define their problems, let's review some research on this topic. Figure 2.0 shows the results of a survey by the Ken Blanchard Companies regarding how organizations rated their top challenges. Consider the items on this list. How do they compare to your own business? What would you add or delete?

Notice how this list focuses on items *external* to the company, such as competitors, hiring pool, technology, and regulation. Also notice how the ratings of each item change over the years. Not surprisingly, the challenges are changing.

Issue	2003	2004	2005	2006	2007	2010
1. Competitve Pressure	71%	67%	63%	60%	65%	62%
2. Growth and Expansion*	n/a	n/a	n/a	53%	60%	52%
3. Skill Shortages	34%	34%	39%	43%	51%	51%
4. Pricing Sensitivity	45%	39%	38%	34%	41%	33%
5. Changing Technology	31%	32%	30%	29%	30%	48%
6. Government Regulation	29%	27%	30%	28%	29%	29%
7. Global Challenges*	n/a	n/a	n/a	22%	24%	35%
8. Industry Consolidation	18%	20%	14%	13%	12%	20%
*Asked in 2006 and 2007 Only						

Figure 2.0–A five-year look at the trends and issues organizations and leaders face, courtesy of the Ken Blanchard Companies, 2007

This is by no means a complete list. In 2007, our own company, Six Disciplines, conducted "What Keeps CEOs Up At Night?" interviews and videotaped one-on-one conversations with business leaders to find out how they described their biggest challenges. Many issues surfaced from these interviews, such as communication, accountability, alignment, leadership transition and control. Following are just a few of the meaningful insights gained from our conversations with these business leaders.

Paul Kramer is the CEO of Kramer Enterprises, a successful, multi-state dry cleaning business that also provides logo apparel as a service to its corporate clients. This is a second-generation family business that employs seventy-five people. Paul was personally at the stage where he was losing interest in his business and acknowledged that he was "kind of coasting along." Here is how he describes what keeps him up at night:

> It was clear to me that if I wanted to stay in business I had to become more organized. I needed a better communication tool. I really don't want to be hanging over people's shoulders being a taskmaster. I would rather be a leader. My biggest problem has been making sure I'm communicating correctly with my leadership team.

Doug Peters is a 23-year veteran CEO of a prominent chamber of commerce:

> We knew what we were supposed to be doing and we knew what the outcome was supposed to be at

the end of the day; but we had no measurement—no
way to chart our progress!

Bob Deardurff is the CEO of a growing international recycling technologies firm:

As we've evolved and gotten larger, it has become
more challenging to
a) effectively communicate without having some
formal planning in place,
b) develop some clear understanding of where we're
going,
c) have alignment of what we need to do through-
out the organization.

The main point is that all business leaders think of their business problems and challenges differently, and the way they view these changes over time. What I'm suggesting is that the Execution Revolution offers a different and more useful way to manage these challenges.

A Change in Perspective

Instead of always focusing on the issue at hand, I'd like to challenge you to change your perspective. The importance of perspective is illustrated by an old tale that's often repeated on the business speaking circuit.

Back in 18th-century England, a thirteen-year-old
boy watched two men working at opposite ends of

a ship that was under construction; both were big strong men wielding axes. He approached the first man and asked him, "What are you doing?" The worker looked up surprised and said, "Are ya' daft?! I'm hewing a log!" The boy then walked to the other end of the ship and asked the second man the same question, "What are you doing?" The second man stopped and looked out across the ocean to the horizon, and said, "I'm building a mighty seagoing schooner that will carry the treasures of the world back to England."[1]

Which of the two shipbuilders would you want to have working for you? While both answers are correct, they demonstrate different ways we have to think about what we're doing. In other words, "What's the challenge?" is another way to ask, "What's the opportunity?" How we formulate the question determines the way we think, and the way we think changes everything.

To achieve a revolution in their execution, business leaders need to reframe their thinking from *cutting logs* to *building ships*. In other words, quit thinking only about solving the current problem, but, instead, think about how to build an organization that's good at solving problems in general—building the capability that's certain to help overcome an uncertain future.

A ship with a crew that knows how to navigate, maintain the engines, and secure the cargo is going to be in a much better position to deal with an unexpected leak than one that can't keep it moving when there are no problems.

How Big Is This Challenge?

Let me ask you a question. In the last five years, how many times has your organization met its annual targets for revenue and profit? Or let's bring it a little closer. How likely is it that you and your organization will meet all or most of *your* goals for this year?

When I was CEO of Solomon Software, we rarely met all—or even most—of our goals. Don't get me wrong. We were a successful company that grew from a start-up to more than 400 people, and we made a fair amount of profit over the years. In our last ten years, we grew six-fold. But we were in a rapidly growing industry, we were reactive, and we struggled hard to learn how to build an organization that could execute well. Maybe we *were* better at it than some organizations but, frankly, we weren't very good. We weren't alone, as you'll see.

A recent McKinsey study concluded that few large global companies outperform their competitors on both revenue growth *and* profitability over a decade.[2] The consulting firm analyzed 1,077 companies according to revenue growth, profitability, and both measures. This study concluded that thirty of these companies were superior, based on growth over this period. Ninety-nine were superior performers by profitability. And only nine (.008 percent) out of 1,077 companies were superior in both categories.

The purpose in highlighting this analysis is to show that achieving such balance and predictability is extremely difficult, and therefore extremely rare. While this fact is viewed as a deterrent to some, it provides insight into an enormous opportunity for building a business that executes more predictably than most.

Following are some observations from the studies of other experts:

- An astounding 90 percent of well-formulated strategies fail due to poor execution.[3]
- Only 5 percent of employees understand their corporate strategy.[4]
- As many as 75 percent of business improvement (change) initiatives to solve these problems fail due to lack of sustainability.[5]
- Only 3 percent of executives think their company is very successful at executing its strategies, while 62 percent think they're only moderately successful, or worse.[6]
- More than 64 percent of C-level executives from 250 midsized to large companies in the United States and the European Union have said that being able to execute, to react quickly to changing business opportunities and technologies, is critical for their success. Yet nearly 80 percent of them said this is nearly impossible to achieve.[7]
- More than 671,000 new businesses open each year, and every year nearly 544,800 businesses close down.[8]

This list is a sobering reminder that execution is a universal challenge. It reminds me of something Michael Porter paraphrased by saying, "It's better to have grade-B strategy and grade-A execution than the other way around."

Execution is even taking precedence over profit and top-line growth as a focus for CEOs around the world. This is according to a global survey of 769 global chief executives from 40 countries, which was released by The Conference Board in October of 2007.[9] When asked to rate their greatest concerns from among 121 different challenges, these chief executives chose *excellence of execution* as their top challenge and keeping consistent execution of strategy by top management as their third greatest concern.

A final argument that execution is business' biggest challenge is the growth of the business improvement industry itself. As business leaders, we're voracious seekers of business improvement ideas in the form of conferences, books, blogs, and training. We want our performance to be better, and we know it *should* be better.

[SUMMARY]

- The biggest problem in business is *not* what most business leaders think it is.
- The biggest challenge is *not* the issue at hand. Planning and executing while at the same time dealing with the unknowns of the real world, *is* the biggest challenge in business.
- Focus on solving the problem that makes all the other problems soluble.
- Developing and executing a strategy that's balanced in growth *and* profitability is extremely difficult and is therefore rare.
- Execution is considered by most business leaders and researchers as a universal challenge.

It's easy to observe that strategy execution is difficult. It's not easy, however, to do something about it. In the next chapter, we'll explore five underlying reasons why strategy execution is so difficult, especially for small and midsized organizations. Any program that is going to work for these organizations must address these issues.

CHAPTER 3

[Why Is It So Difficult?]

" We usually know what to do.
It's just that we don't always
do it.*"*

Why do we know what to do, but don't always do it? Over the past three decades, this is the question I've asked myself more often than any other. Before I go any further, it's probably a good time to reflect on this quote from Lou Holtz, a former college football coach: "When everything is said and done, a lot more is *said*, than done."

I don't want to be guilty of this. I don't just want to leave you with more analysis of the problem. Later on, I'll describe a complete program for doing something about this, and you'll learn what it really takes to move beyond theory to reality.

It's worth a few pages, however, to explore this why question more deeply. Let's start with a study by The Wharton School, in conjunction with the Gartner research firm, as they attempted to gain insight on the same issue, as it relates to larger companies. These institutions asked 243 company leaders to rank items that represented obstacles to the strategy execution process. Figure 3.0 shows how these leaders ranked these obstacles (from greatest obstacle to least):

1. Inability to manage change effectively or to overcome internal resistance to change.
2. Trying to execute a strategy that conflicts with the existing power structure.
3. Poor or inadequate information sharing between individuals or business units responsible for strategy execution.
4. Unclear communication of responsibility and /or accountability for execution decisions or actions.
5. Poor or vague strategy.
6. Lack of feelings of "ownership" of a strategy or execution plans among key employees.
7. Not having guidelines or a matrix to guide strategy-execution efforts.
8. Lack of understanding of the role of organizational structure and design in the execution process.
9. Inability to generate "buy-in" or agreement on critical execution steps or actions.
10. Lack of incentives or inappropriate incentives to support execution objectives.
11. Insufficient financial resources to execute the strategy.
12. Lack of upper-management support of strategy execution.

Figure 3.0–Obstacles to the strategy execution process, joint research, Wharton School, Gartner Group, 2003, All Rights Reserved

Why is strategy execution so difficult? Look at any item on this list. Let's start with the first one, managing change. It *should* be hard: success means growth, growth means change, and change means uncharted territory. If these more obvious changes aren't enough, every individual in your organization is growing and changing, too. Also the industry and your competitors are growing and changing—and you can't afford to be left behind.

"Without change," warns C. William Pollard, Chairman of The ServiceMaster Company, "there is no innovation, creativity, or incentive for improvement. Those who initiate change will have a better opportunity to manage the change that is inevitable."[1]

But, in the midst of all this change, how do you keep everyone on the same page? (My family of five can't even agree where to go for dinner!) When we consider each business individually, we might conclude that the obstacles to executing strategy aren't just complex, they are downright daunting.

"Why" from an SMB Perspective

Surveys like the one discussed earlier provide insight into the way larger companies see the barriers to strategy execution. These perspectives are useful because it has been the larger organizations that have invested the most in attempting to solve such problems. Drawing from my twenty-five years of experience working with small and midsized businesses, complemented by a brutal honesty about my own mistakes, however, I view five major factors that impact small and midsized businesses. Although not the result of a quantitative study, they do represent thousands of hours in the "school of hard knocks."

We Don't Know How to Build an Organization That Executes Well

Organizations are complex systems that are living, breathing, and always changing. Peter Senge, a prominent thought leader in systems thinking said, "Systems thinking is a discipline for seeing wholes. It is a framework for seeing interrelationships rather than things, for seeing patterns of change rather than static snapshots."[2]

Most of us were never trained in the kind of systems thinking necessary to tackle complex systems problems. The majority of us just don't know how to put together all the key steps of strategy, planning, organizational alignment, execution management, innovation, and measurement. And by the time we figure it out, we've moved on to a different set of challenges. In future chapters, we'll explore a wide variety of best practices that have been developed to improve business performance.

One of our clients who ran an insurance agency told me that while he knew how to sell insurance, he didn't know how to get everyone on the same page. He was amazed at how a clear, step-by-step approach allowed his leadership team to head in the same direction. Guess what? The same problems exist at companies with 100, 500 or 1,000 people.

We Fall Into the Trap of "Outside-In" Thinking

Today, television, books, magazines, newspapers, and the Internet keep us flooded with information about what's going on in the world. We become preoccupied with what everyone else is doing, instead of focusing on what's going on *inside* our organizations.

Focusing outward makes us good at being reactive, rather than developing the ability to execute well. The Vail Leadership Institute has the mission of helping individuals develop "inside first" thinking. I advocate this kind of thinking, at both the individual and organizational levels. The Execution Revolution is in fact an *internal* revolution. A revolution focused on changing the way your organization functions on the inside, in other words, controlling the things we can, to be better prepared for the things we can't.

We Are Not in Control (of Much)

We must be realistic about the things we can't control. Economic trends, technological advancement, the competitive landscape, political turmoil, and natural disasters are all beyond our reach.

In August 2007, we were reminded of this in Findlay, Ohio, home of Six Disciplines, when floodwaters from a downpour exceeded the one-hundred-year flood level. Findlay is in northwestern Ohio surrounded by flat farm country, with a small river, the Blanchard, running through town. The photograph in Figure 3.1, however, shows what nine inches of rain did to Findlay in just one day.

Figure 3.1–External factors beyond our control. Downtown Findlay, Ohio USA, after nine inches of rain in one day, (Reuters: Matt Sullivan)

Businesses located in the hurricane corridor may give thought to planning for these types of things, but most businesses in Findlay did not—and for some, it was a fatal blow. Do you have an organization that's trained to plan for the unexpected and to execute these plans quickly?

Usually, It's Easier *Not* To Do What We Know We *Should*

Let's face it. Sometimes execution is boring. Recently my thirteen-year-old son was lobbying for an Xbox 360. We agreed on some goals that would allow him to buy one, which involved doing his schoolwork and achieving certain grades. But within two days, he was shirking his homework. I asked him if he still wanted his Xbox. He said, "Yes."

I asked why he wasn't doing his homework. In a moment of openness, he said, "Dad, I just hate doing it." I appreciated his honesty.

Every leader needs to understand that there's *no one* on earth who wants to do what he or she should do all the time. Let's face it, making the cold calls required to grow sales isn't as easy (or fun) as *planning* to grow sales and visualizing yourself spending the profit. But, as Thomas Edison reminds us, "Vision without execution is a hallucination." If you understand your own tendency and the tendency of others to not do the things we know we should, you'll gain a much better understanding of why execution is such a challenge.

This kind of disinterest can occur even at the top of an organization. One CEO we interviewed was a second-generation owner of a successful business, which employs about seventy-five employees and focuses on three primary markets. He decided he wanted to take his business to another level of excellence. So we conducted an analysis of what his stakeholders (employees and customers) thought of how well the business was performing, compared to their expectations.

What he learned was that his employees were deeply upset with his lack of leadership and commitment to the organization. He was coming in late and leaving the office early to pursue his other interests. And his lack of engagement produced a growing lack of engagement throughout the entire company.

With this input as a motivator, he set out on a systematic program to improve his business, starting with improving himself. Although there were plenty of areas where his business could improve, one immediate result was a reengagement of the owner—a positive condition that quickly spread to all the team members.

While there are many variations on this issue, one of the most anguishing aspects of our humanity is not doing the things we know we should.

Well-respected organizations, such as Weight Watchers, personal fitness coaches, even exclusive membership gyms, all thrive on a key, underlying matrix we'll describe later in this book: the power of accountability. Doing what we know we should requires someone who will keep us on track, to teach, direct, and encourage us to do the things we know we should do—the difficult things that we rarely, if ever, follow through to the finish, if left to our own devices.

But, we're getting ahead of ourselves.

The Growth Paradox

It may seem ironic, but the organization that's good at solving today's challenges will create a new and bigger set of challenges for tomorrow. Why? Because success leads to the need for more: more capital, more people, more leadership, more systems, more competitive intelligence, more of everything. If your company has big plans, you must also prepare for the bigger challenges that will follow.

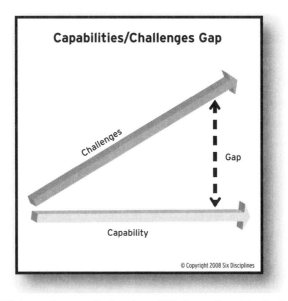

Figure 3.2–Increasing organizational capability in an attempt to shorten the gap of ever-changing, ever-increasing challenges over time

Again using our ship analogy, if you're the captain of a ship that performs well, you're going to eventually be promoted to a bigger ship, one with more surface area for waves to hit and water leaks to occur. This ship brings with it a bigger crew, resulting in more and different challenges ahead. That's what great execution will do for you—it brings you bigger challenges!

This lesson was indelibly imprinted on my mind during an experience at Solomon Software in the mid 1980s. As part of our strategy, we invested early in public relations. As a result, several stories and reviews of our product were published in leading industry publications. We executed that plan almost too well. One January day, a major favorable product review appeared in the most widely read magazine at the time, *PC Magazine*. Within ninety days, our business more than doubled.

In this case, successful execution of our plans caused future execution problems. Our phone lines were overrun. Our production capability was overwhelmed. We were under-staffed for support. It actually took us *years* to recover from executing so well! That's why it's so critical for organizations to continually work on *increasing their capability to execute*. The better they are at executing today, the better they'll need to be in the future! It never stops!

[SUMMARY]

- Strategy execution is hard for a variety of reasons, but it's not rocket science.
- The majority of us don't know how to put together all the key steps of strategy, planning, organizational alignment, execution management, innovation, and measurement.
- Often, we fall into the trap of outside-in thinking, and need to focus on internal things rather than worrying about issues outside of our control.
- We need to keep in mind the control factor: regardless of how well we perform as a business, there are many factors to success we cannot control.

- Sometimes, it's easier *not* to do what we know we *should* do.
- As ironic as it may seem, there is a growth paradox: the organization that's good at solving today's challenges will create a new and bigger set of challenges for itself tomorrow.
- It's critical that organizations continually work on *increasing* their capability to execute.

There's no doubt that it's difficult to learn how to execute strategy well, and to do so consistently over time. In Chapter 4, we'll discuss why the timing is right for small and midsized businesses to approach the challenge of strategy execution in a breakthrough way.

[The Leapfrog Opportunity]

" Conditions are now right to approach the challenge of strategy execution in a radical new way."

Occasionally, circumstances and progress in seemingly unrelated areas combine to create an opportunity for solving old problems in new and exciting ways. One of those breakthrough periods is upon us now, with regard to strategy execution. This *inflection point* has developed primarily because large organizations have made huge investments developing best practices for effective management, strong leadership, and strategy execution. These organizations are of a size where they can and must invest to figure out how to implement holistic quality programs, craft and communicate strategy more effectively, train team members, measure results, and other critical operational issues.

Built on the results of these efforts, we believe the coming Execution Revolution will result in an order-of-magnitude change in cost that will allow SMBs not only to catch up, but to actually leapfrog, larger organizations in their execution management capabilities.

The concept of leapfrogging isn't new. For example, fifty years ago, India lacked the capital and economic development to build a national telephone infrastructure to service all of its homes, thus remaining essentially phoneless for decades. That nation continued to grow stronger economically, however, while cell phone technology emerged. As a result, India is adopting cell phones at an amazing rate and has been able to skip the entire investment in what today is an aging architecture for communications in the U.S.: landline phones.

It's fascinating that situations like this not only can allow markets to catch up, but in some ways, to leap ahead. Nations like the U.S. have had a more complicated time of adopting wireless technology, because we're living with both the old and new approaches. At our house, we still have landline phones, yet everyone also has a cell phone. We're incurring the cost of both for a period, while families in India will not have this expense.

Would we trade places with India? No way! We've enjoyed tremendous benefits from our past progress. On the other hand, should a country like India seize the leapfrog opportunity it has before it? Absolutely!

The same concept of leapfrogging can be applied to many areas. Some nations are leaping from no electricity to solar power as their first source of electrical power, skipping entirely the industrial challenges of fossil and nuclear fuels.

The Lesson for SMBs

So where *is* the leapfrog opportunity for small and midsized businesses? As you've already seen, consistently executing well is an enormous challenge. The tools and enablers for attacking various pieces of the problem are advancing rapidly, but are still fragmented. Large companies have been investing for half a century to develop better solutions for executing strategy. Among their investments have been:

- Quality programs such as Baldrige, Lean, and TQM
- ERP systems for transaction automation and process reengineering
- Knowledge management, data mining tools, and scorecards for performance measurement and management
- New models of training and employee development, including personal and executive coaching

The progress has been amazing and offers us a platform for an inflection point. The problem, however, is that these areas of advancement are broad and deep in themselves, and they come from different providers and thought leaders. In addition, larger companies have had to spend many times the acquisition costs for these systems in order to implement and

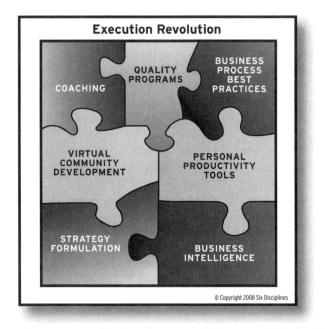

Figure 4.0–Seven areas of business improvement advancements fueling the Execution Revolution

maintain them. SMBs can't realize a sufficient return to justify the high investment levels required to adopt these business best practices. They simply don't have the expertise or the economic resources to make it work.

This is what the Execution Revolution is all about. As you'll see, the pieces are now falling into place to deliver a complete program for SMBs, a program that large companies are trying to build by piecing together many best-of-breed approaches— at an enormous cost.

Leaders of small and mid-sized businesses now have an opportunity to go from almost no system to a new category in the excellence industry—a complete strategy execution program that puts everything needed for balanced strategy execution together in one affordable combination.

We founded Six Disciplines specifically to accelerate the Execution Revolution. Our mission is to study the challenges, understand the barriers, and create and deliver a holistic program that is optimized for strategy execution. The business excellence methodology component of this program is detailed in my first book, *Six Disciplines for Excellence: Building Small Businesses That Learn, Lead and Last.*

Conditions are now right for a next-generation approach. The remaining chapters will describe the essential elements of such a program. But before examining these, let's take a look at what has happened that makes us say, "Now is the time."

It's humbling to realize that all of our progress to date is built on the work of others. Over the past several decades, we've identified seven areas of business improvement advancements that have created the right conditions to piece together the platform for what we're calling the Execution Revolution. (Figure 4.0)

Figure 4.1 shows these seven areas of advancement in an approximate timeline sequence of when they occurred.

I'd ask you to bear with me as we quickly traverse the "acronym soup" of relevant business improvement advancements over the past several decades. Their details are not important. But a broad understanding of what has happened in these areas provides insight into why this revolution could not have occurred until now, and also to make it more obvious why it *must* occur now. As someone aptly put it, "the genie is out of the bottle."

Quality Programs

Long before we heard the phrase "Quality is Job #1," various movements initiated the concept of systematically improving

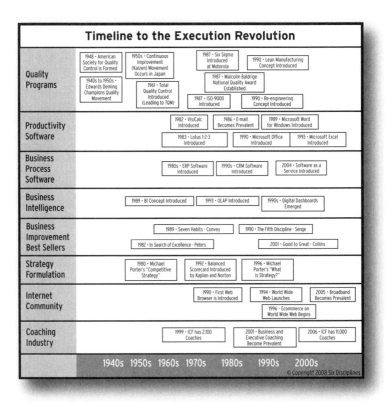

Figure 4.1–Timeline of seven areas of business improvement advancements fueling the Execution Revolution

product quality. Dr. W. Edwards Deming, considered the father of the quality movement, began championing his ideas for a statistical approach to quality in the 1940s and '50s. The United States was the strongest industrial power at the time, but apparently no one saw the need for what he was prescribing. While Deming's message fell on deaf ears in America, Japan desperately needed to rebuild its economy after World War II. Deming taught Japan's top management how to improve design (and thus service), product quality, testing, and sales. In the 1970s, the U.S. market share in the automotive industry began to plummet due to the quality and price gap between U.S. manufacturing and Japanese imports. The economic impact reverberated throughout the U.S., creating the impetus for us to change our ways. This movement continues to bear fruit in many American industries today.

Over the past several decades, a variety of programs, initiatives, and standards have evolved specific to quality improvement, performance, and business excellence. Some of the more prominent approaches include Total Quality Management, the Malcolm Baldrige National Quality Program, Six Sigma, ISO-9000, and Lean Manufacturing. All of these programs have contributed to the Execution Revolution about to occur today.

Personal Productivity Tools

My children are too young to understand this, but there was a time, not too long ago, when you had to write your school papers by hand or type them on a typewriter. Although word processing and spreadsheets were conceived earlier than 1981, the concept of productivity software exploded at the same time IBM introduced its PC (personal computer). It seems silly now, but, at the time, it was a huge shift to think of computers and software as individual-centric, or what we now refer to as personal computing. This marked the beginning of a makeover in the way individuals worked, which led to other developments that transformed the way the world today works, communicates, learns, and entertains itself.

As the breadth of productivity solutions continues to expand, the question arises, "do these systems really increase productivity? Studies by numerous agencies and groups show they do.

> The Congressional Budget Office, the Economic Report of the President, Jorgenson and Stiroh, Whelan, and Macroeconomic Advisers, LLC, find strong evidence that the mid–1990s acceleration in productivity growth was due largely to IT capital deepening among IT users and also to technical advances and innovations made by IT producers.[1]

To support these findings, researchers segmented the entire U.S. economy according to how IT-intensive the various sectors of the economy were in relation to each others. The results (Figure 4.2) show that during this period, industries in the top half of IT investment grew their productivity on an average of

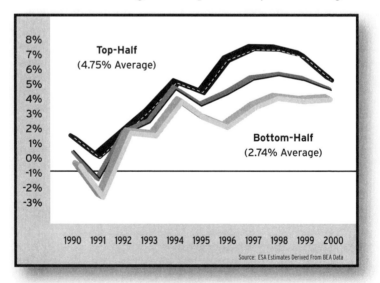

Figure 4.2–GDP growth in top-half and bottom-half in all industries of the U.S. nonfarm business sector, 1989-2000, BEA estimates derived from BEA data

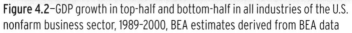

4.76 percent per year and the productivity of the bottom half industries grew at an average of only 2.74 percent.

The essential point here is this: research indicates appropriate investments that leverage technology (these are not just limited to personal productivity software) *do* make a difference in business performance.

Business Process Best Practices

The 1980s is a part of our history that I can speak to from a personal vantage point. In 1980, Jack Ridge, Vernon Strong, and I started Solomon Software, a microcomputer software company that developed accounting software to help businesses handle payables, receivables, billing, inventory management, financial reporting, order processing, and project management. These were exciting times! The microcomputer software market was exploding with a variety of business software programs: spreadsheets, word processing, and presentation graphics, to name just a few in addition to accounting software. To give you a sense of how rapid this personal technology movement was at the time, Figure 4.3 shows the Editor's Choice product review of Solomon III, our accounting software program. This review appeared in the January 1985 issue *PC Magazine*, the leading personal computing magazine of its time. The impact of this Editor's Choice product review more than doubled our business in just ninety days!

The US SMB market was embracing business software and technology at unprecedented rates. But what were these businesses really embracing? To a great extent, it was

Figure 4.3–PC Magazine's Price Waterhouse Review of Accounting Software, featuring the Editor's Choice, Solomon III (1985)[2]

a doing-what-everyone-else-is-doing sort of bandwagon. What savvy organizations were *really* looking for, however, was a better way to do business. Over time, I determined that Solomon Software really wasn't in the software business. It was in the business of figuring out how businesses work and then encoding those best practices into software. The goal of our business was actually to help other businesses execute mainstream business processes more efficiently, more predictably, and with fewer errors.

In the process of developing best practices for common business transactions, the accounting software market transitioned into a broader and deeper class of software known as ERP, or Enterprise Resource Planning. ERP software focuses on automating and streamlining common business transactions, which significantly assists initiatives designed to improve execution.

Figure 4.4 illustrates the magnitude of this overall ERP market movement, showing that the total investment in software since 1970 approaches $200 billion in the U.S. alone! The point here is not about the growth of software, but *the growth in knowledge about how businesses work*. It is this stage of evolution that is significant in preparing the SMB world for the Execution Revolution.

Business Intelligence

During the past few decades, ERP systems that provided transaction-based business solutions have thrived. At the same time, separate-but-related industries were spawned to address the increased usage of all of this newly mined business data.

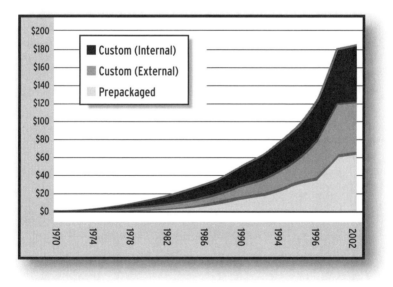

Figure 4.4–Larger business investments in software, in billions of dollars, 1970-2002, BEA data

Business Intelligence (BI) is a relatively new discipline. Typically, BI uses large, distributed relational databases for storage, data mining, data warehousing, and online analytic processing (OLAP), and so on.

Performance Management (PM) is a field of expertise that attempts to integrate a company's processes in order to better understand its priorities. Performance management involves consolidating data from various transaction sources (for example, ERP and CRM), querying and analyzing this data, and, perhaps most importantly, putting the results from this effort into practice.

Industry experts define BI and PM as the tools, applications, and processes that help companies to improve their performance. Larger companies that adopt some aspect of business intelligence and performance management are better able to gauge customer satisfaction, control customer trends, and influence shareholder value. Performance management solutions provide key performance indicators that help companies monitor the efficiency of projects and employees against operational targets, thereby, improving strategy execution.

Strategy Formulation

A highly visible by-product of BI and PM best practices is the scorecard. The scorecard monitors key measures much like a report card monitors academic achievement, to show an organization how well it's performing. Scorecards can be maintained in a report or a spreadsheet, handwritten on a whiteboard, or graphically displayed on a digital dashboard (a collection of key business indicators from various sources) using charts, gauges and stoplights.

Any discussion about business intelligence, performance management and strategy formulation advancements and innovations is remiss without pointing out the contributions of balanced scorecards. A balanced scorecard is a strategic, measurement-based management system, originated by Harvard professors Robert Kaplan and David Norton in 1992. Its goal is to translate a mission statement and overall business strategy into specific, quantifiable goals, and to measure the organization's performance toward reaching those goals. Balanced scorecards are one of the few proven tools that companies operating in Quadrants I and II use to help them craft and communicate better strategy.

Most of the other best practice advancements and business improvement innovations have focused on improving

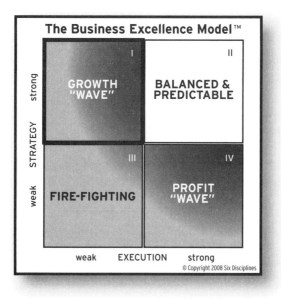

efficiency—doing things right, and doing things better, faster and cheaper. Formulating strategy, on the other hand, is about *doing the right things*.

Balanced scorecards go beyond the traditional financial indicators monitored by business intelligence software. They also help measure operational efficiency, employee performance, customer satisfaction, and financial performance. The primary benefit of scorecards is better alignment of long-term strategies with short-term activities.

Over the past decade, the balanced scorecard has become a widely advocated management tool that has been closely associated with business best practices in larger companies. Its appeal is also reflected in reported estimates that somewhere between 50 to 70 percent of Fortune 1000 firms use it in some form or another.

Since the goal of the balanced scorecard is to align business activities with strategy and monitor performance toward strategic goals over time, the implication for small and mid-sized businesses is clear: implementation of some form of balanced scorecard component is vital to an overall strategy execution program.

Virtual Community Development

"Think of these strategic management best practices as a core competency for an organization. These practices can be identified, codified, and thus **shared with others**, helping to move strategic management from an art to a science.[3]**"**

We debated long and hard about what to call this trend. A main contender was "communication," as in virtual communication development. But we finally decided that the increase in communication capability—enabled by the Internet, PCs and email—is actually in the power of the *communities* they have enabled, and the shared learning that can take place as a result of these.

In the history of humanity, communities have been based primarily on physical location, family, and heritage. The term community has stood for how people lived and learned together, sharing values, economic dependencies, and even protection. But today, we're witnessing the beginning of a unique development: the power of *virtual communities*. It's a new kind of freedom, the freedom to associate yourself or your organization with others, regardless of where they are located.

Communities are formed by people who spend time together—even if only virtually. Figure 4.5 reveals an amazing statistic: people around the world are spending ten to twenty hours *a week* online, a trend that's continuing to increase. This is a huge shift in the way we use our time—all in less than ten years.

The Internet has changed both the economics and the delivery mechanism for how communities start, connect, communicate, and innovate. Virtual communities spring up daily. As we'll see later, the Internet has eliminated locality or geography as a requirement for being involved in a community, enabling any group of like-minded individuals and organizations to work together to accelerate learning and growing.

The number of online communities, and community members in them, continues to grow. According to a 2007 Pew Internet study, 84 percent of Internet users belong to some kind of online community.[4] Furthermore, close to 50 million

Country	Mean Number of Hours Online Per Week
China	17.9
Japan	13.9
South Korea	12.7
Canada	12.3
U.S.	11.4
Mexico	9.2
France	9.1
Germany	8.9
Brazil	8.8
U.K.	8.6
Russia	5.7
India	4.4

Source: Ipsos, 2006

Figure 4.5–Global weekly Internet usage time by country, November-December 2005, Ipsos Public Affairs, 2006

people have joined some type of community they discovered while browsing online.

Coaching

Coaching is a mainstay of corporate organizational development and has experienced a long evolution since its beginnings in the late 1950s. Growth of the coaching industry was rapid in the 1980s, when it was hailed as a management tool for improving work performance and for building teams.

In a 1996 *Newsweek* article, Thomas Leonard, considered to be one of the fathers of business coaching, estimated there were 1,000 coaches nationwide.[5] In 1999, the first year that member numbers were recorded, the International Coach Federation (ICF) had 2,122 members. By 2008, ICF membership exceeded 14,000 (Figure 4.6).

Executive coaching services are an extension of the coaching industry, and their growth in popularity can be explained by our modern-day business environment. Executives are required to manage greater complexity, risk, and pressure at a faster pace than ever before. In order to perform effectively, they need a way to accelerate learning, improve performance, and modify behavior accordingly. Of the executives who have worked with an executive coach, 93 percent reported that it was a positive, sometimes life-changing, experience.

Despite the preference by some business coaches to conduct their services by phone, clients express a strong preference to do so in person. As Figure 4.7 shows, an overwhelming 96

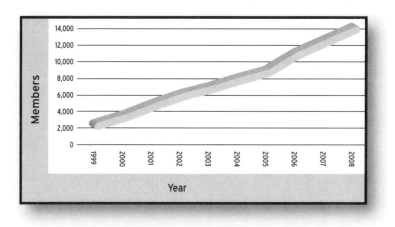

Figure 4.6–International Coach Federation membership growth

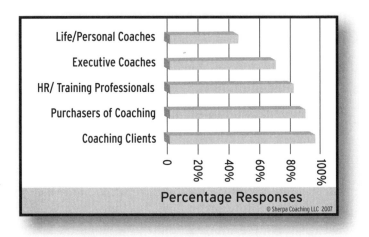

Figure 4.7–How different groups rate the effectiveness of in-person coaching, Sherpa Coaching, LLC, 2007

percent of those who had worked with an executive coach say *in-person coaching* is the best.[6]

Unlike stand-alone training programs that cover a particular issue or topic, coaching is an ongoing, consistent process that focuses on specific performance-related goals. As an *Ivy Business Journal* article expressed in 2000:

> Coaching simply speeds up a process of change that would most likely occur anyway, if an individual had enough time. Without a coaching program that forces a client to focus and make time, people sometimes miss the real issues they need to focus on.[7]

In 2004, a *Harvard Business Review* report summarized the reasons why executive coaching works:

- Executive coaching engages with people in customized ways that acknowledge and honor their individuality.

- The essentially human nature of coaching is what makes it work—and also what makes it nearly impossible to quantify.
- In most organizations, lasting change usually occurs slowly, one person at a time, gaining momentum as more people buy in.
- To accelerate change and make it stick, they recommend systematically coordinating one-on-one coaching interventions that serve a larger objective.
- There's another advantage of starting at the top: once senior leaders have changed their behavior, it's easier for them to influence the rest of the workforce to do the same.[8]

Related to the executive coaching industry are CEO advisory groups such as Vistage International, TAB (The Alternative Board), and, more recently, online CEO groups such as PeerSightOnline.com. These advisory groups use a peer CEO coaching framework to offer support and advice among their members. As such, the participants, themselves, are essentially CEOs helping other CEOs. In a way, it's peer-to-peer business coaching.

There's much to be said for this approach, since as peers, fellow CEOs can offer a beneficial "been there . . . done that" perspective. There's a level of trust and belonging within these CEO peer groups that is difficult to gain in other ways.

Business coaching has emerged as an industry that has proven its value. The model of bringing outside expertise and accountability to organizations and individuals within organizations works. As such, it is one of the core tenets upon which the Execution Revolution will be built.

[SUMMARY]

■ Conditions are currently right to approach strategy execution in a radical new way.

■ Seven key areas of business improvement advancements are fueling the Execution Revolution: quality programs, business process best practices, personal productivity tools, business intelligence, strategy formulation, virtual community development, and business coaching.

In Chapter 5, we'll pull all the pieces together, so that you can see how the business improvement innovations during the past few decades fit together into a next-generation approach to strategy execution.

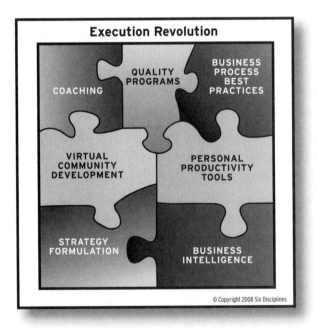

CHAPTER 5

[Requirements for a Next-Generation Program]

" Any next-generation solution that stands a chance of taking organizations to the next level of business excellence—and sustaining it—must address our human nature and help us overcome our frequent failure to do the things we know we should do."

In researching how to build a sustainable strategy execution program, we've uncovered three major barriers that have to be overcome if the program is to be successful. They are insufficient expertise, prohibitive economics, and simple human nature. We've determined that these three barriers are actually the major design requirements any truly effective strategy execution program must be able to address.

Most business leaders we've talked to have tried various approaches to achieving business improvement (e.g., consultants, seminars, books, tapes, and software) and, for whatever reason, have not been able to make the results of these efforts last, or to make them "stick." Appreciating the expertise, economic and human nature hurdles, then, is key to understanding why we've designed the strategy execution program the way we have (see Chapter 6 for a complete program description).

The Expertise Hurdle

For such a program to work in small and midsized businesses, it must help the organizations using it to deal with the breadth of expertise required. As discussed earlier, many of the best practices in business management are the result of decades of trial and error in larger companies

Figure 5.0 summarizes the many areas of expertise that large companies invest in to better manage their business and improve their ability to execute.

Actually, this diagram only represents a partial list of the breadth *and* depth of expertise required to be above average in business performance. The real effort is massive and usually significantly underestimated. Large companies not only have knowledgeable people with the necessary breadth of expertise, but frequently have whole departments focused on each of these areas. This leads to a three-fold managerial challenge: finding and keeping people with the required expertise; staying current with the latest developments in all of these separate areas; and figuring out how to integrate these best practices into an integrated and effective strategy.

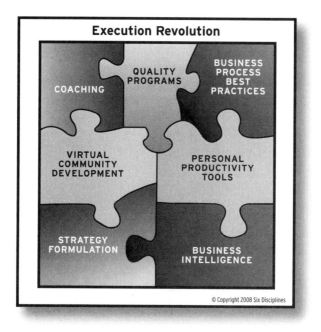

Figure 5.0–Areas of expertise that large companies invest in

What most who lead growing organizations fail to understand—until they are having severe problems—is that the needs of their organizations are changing and they don't realize it. They're suffering from what I described in my book *Six Disciplines for Excellence* as creeping misalignment.

Creeping misalignment occurs every day, often in very small ways, as the organization changes. Again, phone answering is an example. When a business gets started, the phone-answering approach is typically pretty simple. First, whoever's available answers the phone and can easily tell who's in and who's not. Phone messages are stuck on the appropriate person's desk somewhere. At this stage the person calling never knows who's going to answer the phone. As the business grows, call volume increases. More mistakes get made in message handling and people get tired of being interrupted to answer other peoples' calls. Eventually, the pain gets so great that an administrator is hired and given responsibility to answer the phone. Since the office is still fairly small, the administrator knows who's in and who's not, approximately when they'll return, etc. This approach provides a consistent voice and some friendly, personal service and attention to the caller. As the business keeps growing, however, the administrator can't handle the call volume. An automated system is installed with voice mail. It works okay, if callers know who they want to talk to. The caller gets a standardized experience, but it's less personal and a little discomforting if there's an urgent issue.

This example illustrates creeping misalignment. As the business changes, the "current" approach slowly becomes less aligned with other goals of the company. As a result, it becomes an increasing drag on the success of the company until corrected.[1]

To produce lasting results, any complete strategy execution program has to somehow help the organizations that use it to cope with the wide range of expertise required to employ the appropriate best practices that are available. It must also help these organizations recognize that this body of knowledge will keep growing and changing.

The Economics Hurdle

For the Execution Revolution to occur in small and midsized businesses, the acquisition cost equation for adopting a strategy execution program based on proven best practices must be proportionate to its outcome. No program can be practical if the cost to implement it is prohibitive.

Larger businesses spend about two percent of sales to maintain their IT operations. Assuming this same rate of investment, a $10 million company would invest $1 million over a five-year period and a $1 billion company would invest $100 million. Clearly, there is much more opportunity to invest in best practices when the budget is large.

Remember that investments in software and technology are, in essence, investments in more effective business best practices. Small and midsized businesses simply don't have the economies of scale to invest in the array of technologies and programs described in Chapter 4, not to mention the expertise to integrate and utilize it effectively.

The sobering conclusion is that mastering even one of these business improvement disciplines requires a substantial investment. None of them comes cheaply, and there are no shortcuts. In the past, taking your company from good to great in one or more of these disciplines required money, time (maybe decades) and expertise (in-house experts or external consultants). And until now, these developments were only affordable to big business.

Additionally, larger companies can afford (and must spend) *multiples* of the original technology purchase price in order to integrate these technologies with their existing technical infrastructures. Traditionally, for every dollar spent on packaged software, larger organizations invest another two dollars on custom integration to make it all fit together.

The economic hurdle for SMBs really struck me during a business improvement conference in North Carolina where I met a woman who was *Vice President of Performance Excellence* for a large health care provider. While I was encouraged to see the organization's emphasis on excellence—it had a *vice president* dedicated to the concept—I realized that the same level of commitment doesn't exist in SMB organizations. Not because this expertise isn't needed, but because it's unaffordable.

The economic limitations for small and midsized businesses became even more apparent to me during a conversation with a strategy consultant at a performance management conference in Chicago. This successful professional was excited to tell me all about the latest trends in performance management software, balanced scorecards, and the like. When I asked him what he could do to help small and midsized businesses, his reaction was short and to the point: *"Frankly, I only target companies with a bare minimum of $100 million in annual revenue—anything less and this approach is not affordable."* And his firm only focused on one or two of the seven areas of business improvement we described in Chapter 4.

Clearly, any strategy execution program developed for small and midsized businesses must consider how to deliver the expertise and technology required at an economic level that these organizations can afford. The only way this can be achieved is by integrating these essential components of the program—in a complete solution—and deliver them using an innovative distribution model.

The Human Nature Hurdle

> **"**First . . . human beings all over the earth have this
> curious idea that they ought to behave in a certain
> way . . . Secondly . . . they do not in fact behave in that
> way . . . . These two facts are the foundation of all clear
> thinking about ourselves and the universe we live in. **"**

> —*C.S. Lewis, Author, Scholar*

Now, for the toughest hurdle of all: people. Let me repeat a story I told in my first book to show you what I mean.

> The idea behind Six Disciplines crystallized for me at the Grouse Mountain Lodge in Whitefish, Montana on a warm, cloudless day in July 2001. I was a guest speaker at a business improvement conference, and during the frequent outdoor breaks I asked the participants what they were learning and whether the conference was useful to them. Thinking about my questions, Eric, a conference attendee, looked beyond me to the mountains in the backdrop of the lodge. After a few moments of reflection, he plainly stated what I'd heard from several other small business leaders: "This material is outstanding . . . but I probably won't be doing anything about it two years from now."

After hearing this comment, it finally dawned on me that in the pursuit of excellence, figuring out the right things to do isn't nearly as difficult as continuing to do them over the long term. The depth of this challenge sank in when I realized how pervasive the problem of knowing versus doing really is. It was then that I became passionately committed to the idea of Six Disciplines. Over the past several years, I've continued to direct that passion toward helping businesses sustain their pursuit of excellence. And we found that the best way to do it was to help them build their ability to execute strategy.

One of the most persistent challenges we face as humans is to narrow the gap between *knowing* what needs to be done, and actually *doing* what needs to be done. In fact, as business leaders, we collectively know quite a bit about what needs to be done. We've read the books, taken seminars, and listened to management gurus. We've even earned business degrees in understanding *what needs to be done*. Yet the challenge to somehow bridge this gap continues.

Think about this knowing-versus-doing gap in your own life, and how it relates to dieting, for example. Or let's consider the 40-year old business called Weight Watchers, which generated worldwide revenues of $3.0 billion in 2006. The core of the Weight Watchers approach is the weekly meeting that promotes weight loss through education and group support, in conjunction with a flexible, healthy diet. Each week, 1.5 million people attend approximately 50,000 Weight Watchers meetings, led by 15,000 classroom leaders around the world.

In the Weight Watchers business model, the counselors talk to you, weigh you, and educate you through group involvement about food and exercise. Essentially, they give you the kind of advice that you probably learned in grade school. And, you pay them for it! In my experience, it's money well spent, because when I stop going to the weekly meetings, I gain the weight back. My point in this example is simple. What happens at Weight Watchers are things we already know how to do—in other words, we already know to eat right, exercise and weigh ourselves. Yet on our own, do we?

Frequently, I hear my clients tell stories about how they spent large sums of money on comprehensive studies of their businesses—studies that generated strategy formulation and even summary action plans, as well as a complete consulting engagement. And then they bemoan how these strategic planning binders are sitting on the shelf collecting dust! They tell me all about the business improvement books they've read, the seminars they've taken, and the conferences they've attended. And then they wince at having spent so much time and money learning things they already know—with nothing to show for it. And most realize—it's their own fault.

Any approach that stands a chance of taking organizations to the next level of business excellence—and helping them stay there—must address our human nature and help us overcome our frequent failure to do the things we know we should do.

When looking squarely at what is required to execute consistently, another dimension of human nature that needs to be considered is resistance to change. Most of us resist change, unless it's our own idea. Or, as Leo Tolstoy put it: *"Everyone thinks of changing the world, but no one thinks of changing himself."*

Since what is being advocated in the Execution Revolution is a new way to work on your business, one thing needs to be stated clearly: the Execution Revolution requires *change*. And we must admit to ourselves that *resistance to change is a definite part of the human nature hurdle*. Research by John

Kotter, a Harvard Business School professor and author who has studied the challenge of change for decades, reveals that 75 percent of change initiatives fail because the organization is unsuccessful in managing the human reaction to change.[2] In spite of all the books and attention that change gets, organizations don't seem to be getting substantially better at managing or leading change initiatives. According to Kotter: *"Changing people's behavior: It's the most important challenge for businesses trying to compete in a turbulent world. The central issue is never strategy, structure, culture, or systems. The core of the matter is always about changing the behavior of people."*

Clearly, this assertion fits squarely within the original premise of the Execution Revolution: planning and executing and at the same time, while dealing with the unknowns of the real world, is still the biggest challenge in business. It requires change and that's hard—very hard.

Everyone knows we are each uniquely different, with our own experiences, beliefs, strengths and weaknesses. Helping a single individual maximize his or her potential is a challenge in itself. Putting together an organization that maximizes the *collective potential* of its entire workforce is orders of magnitude more difficult. And the more successful the organization becomes, the more challenging this process becomes.

Success drives growth. Growth leads to an increase in the workforce. And more people mean more individual differences. And as long as the organization performs well, this cycle never stops. Any enduring program for strategy execution must help organizations cope with the ever-changing dynamic of how people interact and communicate. This doesn't mean just simply putting up with differences, but learning how to engage and leverage the collective potential of every individual in the organization.

Based on my experience of evaluating business organizations, another challenging and underestimated component of human nature is communication. The book of Genesis in the Bible tells the story of a group of people trying to build a tower to Heaven. Partway through the project, God observed, "They are one people and since they have the same language... nothing which they purpose to do will be impossible for them."(Genesis 10:1–11:26) Later, God concluded that the way to thwart these people from working together to reach their goal was to confuse their language so they couldn't understand each other. This passage illustrates the role of communication in an organization: when people do not understand each other, nothing gets accomplished. But when communication is clear, there's little that can't be achieved.

Business execution will never improve unless we business leaders take the challenge of communication more seriously. How many times have you told someone something that you thought was clear, only to find out later this person walked away with a completely different understanding of what you meant? As I like to say, "Words are a poor approximation for meaning."

George Bernard Shaw once quipped, "The biggest problem with communication is the illusion that it has taken place." The larger the organization, the greater this illusion becomes. As organizations grow, so do the challenges of communication. In fact, the challenges grow exponentially faster than the headcount.

Organizations respond to this increased complexity by creating business units, divisions, departments, groups, teams, and so on. In other words, more layers. Add to this challenge the fact that experts believe fully 55 percent of all human communication takes place through non-verbal body language. In smaller organizations, it becomes easier to appreciate the advantage of being able to gather everyone together in one place, quickly and easily.

In my lifetime, I've hired more than 1,000 people and have personally managed dozens of them. To a person, they all shared one universal desire: the need to have their working lives count for something meaningful, to work at something that has a real purpose.

Personally, I appreciate the words of the signers of the Declaration of Independence when they said, "we are endowed by our Creator." What I'm referring to is that we are endowed with a deep-seated desire to use our God-given talents and abilities to build families, businesses, schools, and governments. We are equipped with an innate desire to create art, music, literature, and laws—to manage the resources around us. It is these needs, desires, and hungers that give us the drive to do something meaningful, to do something that has purpose.

For an organization to achieve its potential, its workforce must understand the purpose of the organization, where it's headed, and have an appreciation for the role everyone has in helping it get there. If our workforces operate with passion and conviction, they'll propel our organizations toward their goals and increase their ability to sustain the balance between strategy and execution.

[SUMMARY]

- In order to build a sustainable strategy execution program in small and midsized businesses, three major barriers or hurdles need to be overcome: insufficient *expertise*, prohibitive *economics*, and simple *human nature*.

- While larger companies have knowledgeable people with the necessary expertise in business improvement disciplines, small and midsized organizations don't have equal access to such a wide array of expertise.

- Developing mastery in even just one business improvement discipline requires a substantial investment. None of this comes cheap, and there are no shortcuts.

- Any strategy execution program developed for small and midsized businesses must consider how to deliver the expertise and technology required in a way that makes sense economically for these enterprises. The only way this kind of change in economics can be achieved is by integrating the essential components of such a program into a complete solution, and delivering them using an innovative distribution model.

- One of the most persistent challenges we face as humans is to narrow the gap between *knowing* what needs to be done, and actually *doing* what needs to be done.

- Other human nature hurdles to be overcome include our resistance to change, our unique differences, our need to communicate effectively, and our need for purpose in our lives, including meaningful work.

At last we are ready to describe the solution to the biggest challenge in business—a next gneration program for building businesses that execute strategy. Let's move on to Chapter 6.

[The First Complete Strategy Execution Program]

" Our field research has shown us that singular piece-meal approaches just don't last. What is needed is a complete program that addresses the major hurdles in front of us.*"*

The critical question for every business leader is, "How do I build an organization that consistently executes its strategy?" Or to rephrase the question using the business excellence model, "How can we spend the maximum amount of time in Quadrant II, balancing the right directional choices with the ability to *get there*."

The answer: it takes a *complete program*. The reasons other approaches do not last is that they are missing key elements.

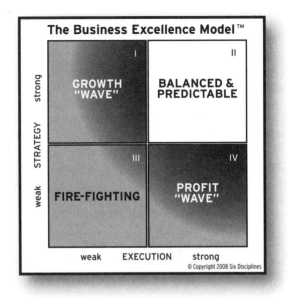

Technology alone is not enough. Training, by itself, is not adequate. Simply reading best-selling books won't do it. New leadership by itself is not the answer. Retaining better people won't make the critical difference. Hiring an executive coach by itself will not overcome this challenge. No, the answer lies in taking a more profoundly holistic approach.

Our field research has shown us that singular piece-meal approaches just don't last. Sustainability, *the capacity of an organization to maintain the necessary balance between strategy and execution,* and doing so while overcoming the hurdles described in Chapter 5, requires a complete program consisting of four tightly-integrated elements, shown in Figure 6.0:

- *A Repeatable Methodology* to drive organizational learning and understanding
- *Accountability Coaching* to nurture and nudge to stay the course

- *An Execution System* to engage everyone, ever real-time alignment
- *Community Learning* to share and reinforce best practices and accelerate learning

Different experts may use alternate terms for these concepts, but rather than fixating on terminology for now, it's better to focus on understanding the underlying principles. Let's look closer at each of these four components.

A Repeatable Methodology

Several years ago, I asked the owner of a successful engineering firm what the formula was for building a top-notch building.

Figure 6.0–The first complete strategy execution program

He said it takes three elements: (1) a good understanding of the purpose of the building; (2) an experienced design team; and (3) strong construction management to assure that the structure was built according to the design. When I asked if he followed a standard approach for doing all of these, he answered, "Absolutely!" and pointed to a thick binder detailing the key steps for estimating costs, designing projects and managing construction. When I asked where this process came from, he said it was the result of his years of education and experience, starting with college, followed by ten years working on many different projects. It took this kind of background to understand the process well enough to do it successfully.

"After thirty years of doing this," he concluded, "we're still learning how to do it better every day. We're continually learning how to take advantage of the latest technology and construction methods. It never stops."

What struck me at that moment was the similarity between building a *building* and building a *business*. That thought led me to ask him if he was as good at building his business as he was at building buildings. He paused, and then flatly stated, "No way." I inquired whether he was following any process for "building his business."

He looked at me quizzically and asked what I meant. I responded by telling him, "A business is similar to a building. It requires purpose, careful design, management, and maintenance. Instead of being made of bricks and mortar, and electrical, heating and lighting systems, a business is made of people, strategy, business processes, technology, and expertise. And just as in engineering a building, engineering a business takes enormous skill, broad experience and a commitment to continuous learning to keep up with change."

I pointed to his engineering methodology binder and asked whether he had a similar methodology for building his business. He said he didn't know there was one. I asked him how successful his organization would be without following the building methodology he'd just described. His answer was, "We're *totally* dependent upon it. By repeating this process on every project, we get better and better at learning how to apply it. If we didn't have the methodology, our learning would be much slower, and our quality wouldn't be as good. In fact, when we get overly confident in our own skills, we sometimes get sloppy and skip a step. Usually it causes a problem that surfaces much later in the project, but ends up costing a great deal more to rectify." I nodded my head, and reassured him that I knew what he meant, from my *own* experience.

I've had similar conversations with leaders of many different kinds of businesses: physicians, contractors, and manufacturers, to name just a few. They all have well-defined approaches to customer excellence, which they consistently deliver to their client. But none of them have a repeatable methodology for setting purpose, evaluating strategy, developing plans, aligning their people and processes, and daily engaging all their team members to execute those plans! Since their doors continue to be open, they obviously have organizations that are functioning adequately. The million-dollar question is: how much *better* would their organizations be if these leaders had a step-by-step approach for building their *business*, as they do for building their product or service?

Both in our research and through trial and error, we discovered that the foundation of a complete program balancing strategy and execution is having *a well-defined, repeatable methodology*. The methodology must include the basic processes every organization needs to go through in order to continue in business: strategy, planning, organizing, execution, innovation, and learning.

The purpose of such a methodology is to accelerate the learning of proven best practices for building any business. This learning never stops. Without such a step-by-step approach, learning becomes nothing more than an endless process of missteps, trial and error, and firefighting. We'll walk through an example of the kind of methodology I'm referring to in Chapter 7. Because we didn't find a single methodology that seemed suitable or complete for small and midsized businesses, we developed our own, the Six Disciplines® methodology. It's not critical to use *our* methodology, but it is critical to use *some* systematic and repeatable approach.

But be forewarned: a methodology by itself is not enough!

Accountability Coaching

The second key ingredient for an enduring approach to business excellence is *accountability coaching*. Both words in this phrase are key. The accountability factor is a requirement because *someone* needs to be off the field rather than in the game: someone who's objective about what's going on. Coaching is vital because, just as the need for practice never stops, the need for coaching never stops. Even great athletes like Lance Armstrong and Tiger Woods continuously use sports coaches to help improve the details and direction of their performance.

One clarification, however: there are many different types of coaches—executive, personal, fitness, and so forth. An accountability coach is specially trained and certified in the repeatable methodology and he or she guides an organization

in its use of that methodology. It's this coach that provides insight on where to start, how fast to go, and what to do next, according to the uniqueness of each business. It's the coach who provides encouragement and advice, and who brings a broader perspective, drawing from years of experience working with other teams and companies.

Drawing an analogy from the physical sciences, the second law of thermodynamics, the law of entropy, holds that any closed system will eventually decline or become completely disorganized unless more energy is put into the system. I used this example in my first book, *Six Disciplines for Excellence*: an ice cube removed from a freezer will melt, unless energy is added from the freezer's cooling unit. Another example is my daughter's bedroom. Unless some energy from outside her room is applied (her mother's firm tone of voice), that room will not get any more orderly on its own (in fact, it'll quickly descend further into chaos).

We observe frequently in our research about how organizations are subject to *organizational* entropy. If disorganized companies ever make it into Quadrant II, they quickly drift back out of it, lacking strong self-discipline and a systematic approach. In addition, they'd need the benefit of some outside energy: an experienced, veteran coach who can provide accountability and perspective.

We've also learned that accountability coaching is most effective when it's done face-to-face. We believe this is because successful coaching relationships are based on a high level of trust. This must be someone who you believe has your best interest at heart and will tell you the truth. This kind of relationship is only developed over time and in person. This view is absolutely contrary to the trend in today's Internet world, toward increased self-service, or a do-it-yourself mentality.

Again, the first essential element in a complete program for improving an organization's ongoing ability to execute strategy is a repeatable methodology. The second element we discussed is accountability coaching. But even these powerful tools, by themselves, are not enough to make a strategy execution program sustainable. Two more pieces of the puzzle are also required.

An Execution System

During our research, the two requirements for a complete strategy execution program (a repeatable methodology and accountability coaching) became obvious fairly quickly. The third requirement, however, an *execution system*, became clear only after we had observed organizations attempting to apply the first two.

We learned that the methodology provided tremendous value to company leadership in organizing its planning efforts, resulting in a highly engaged leadership team. This confirmed that a well-defined approach with the right people in the room produced solid results quickly. But we also found that those who were not involved in the strategic planning process were not getting nearly the value from the business-building program.

As we experimented with approaches for increasing total engagement at *all* levels of an organization, we realized that

The First Complete Strategy Execution Program

VI.
STEP
BACK
Learn

I.
DECIDE
WHAT'S
IMPORTANT
Strategy

V.
INNOVATE
PURPOSEFULLY
Innovate

- Repeatable Methodology
- Accountability Coaching
- **Execution System**
- Community Learning

II.
SET GOALS
THAT LEAD
Plan

IV.
WORK
THE PLAN
Execute

III.
ALIGN
SYSTEMS
Organize

© Copyright 2008 Six Disciplines

everyone needs to be involved in the planning (to an appropriate degree) and everyone needs to connect his or her own activities to the plans of the company. Finally, we realized that we could use technology to help workers make real-time decisions about what work they should do, in what order, and how to prioritize interruptions and unexpected requests for their time and attention.

This whole process of marrying company plans with individual management of daily activities is what we refer to as an *execution system.* An execution system is not easy to deliver, but it points to the future of application development models that will blend many of the best practices developed over the past thirty years. This element of the program is key to understanding why the time is now for the Execution Revolution. The convergence of the software, training, coaching, and strategy tools, all optimized for Internet delivery, have not been economically or technically feasible until now. We'll explore the ramifications of execution systems in Chapter 9. Now, let's provide an overview of the final component.

Community Learning

The fourth and final part of a complete program for a complete strategy execution program is *community learning.* This component helps address the breadth of expertise and the economic barriers required for successful program implementation.

As previously discussed, small and midsized organizations do *not* have an economic model or size capable of supporting the expertise required to research, prove, and integrate the

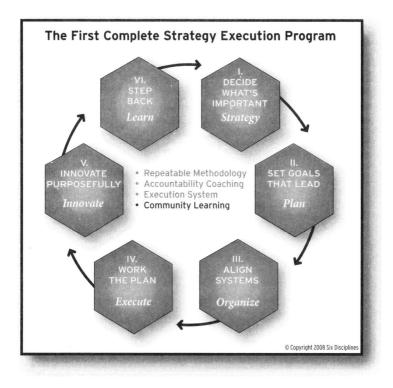

latest business best practices. In addition, with the business world changing so rapidly, no program in the SMB market can endure unless it is self-renewing and continually evolving.

Community learning derives its synergy from the other elements of the program. The rate of learning is accelerated by a group of people sharing a common repeatable methodology, where they all use the same terminology and techniques. It's also accelerated by the coaching program, where accountability coaches pool their experiences applying the methodology in different business scenarios.

The goal of these four program elements working together is to engage every worker, every day, in proactively making more aligned decisions, rather than reactively fixing misalignments later. This, too, is a learning objective for the entire company. Each organization becomes a type of learning community inside a bigger community consisting of all organizations that are practicing the program.

[SUMMARY]

- Spending the maximum amount of time in Quadrant II of The Business Excellence Model takes a complete strategy execution program. Piece-meal approaches simply don't last.
- Sustainability, the capacity of an organization to maintain the necessary balance between strategy and execution and doing so while overcoming the hurdles described in Chapter 5 requires a complete program consisting of four tightly-integrated elements: a repeatable methodology, accountability coaching, an execution system, and community learning.

From this brief overview, it may not be obvious, but the first component of the complete program—the repeatable methodology—is a blueprint of which best-practices are to be adopted in the organization. The other three elements (accountability coaching, execution system and community learning) are *how* the organization implements and sustains practice of the methodology.

These components working together form the complete program upon which the Execution Revolution is based. Never before have small and midsized businesses had the proven best practices and technological foundation to build on. Never before have they had the ability to systematically attack their biggest challenge: *to grow the capability of their organizations to execute strategy and handle the inevitable surprises that come as a normal course of business.*

In the next four chapters, we'll explore the significance of each of these elements in more detail. And in our final two chapters, we'll address the power and synergy of how they all work together.

CHAPTER 7

[A Repeatable Methodology]

" A single, repeatable
methodology, optimized for the
disciplines of setting strategy,
developing plans, organizing
and aligning resources,
managing execution, enabling
innovation and encouraging
organizational learning is
the foundation of a complete
strategy execution program.*"*

In this chapter, we're going to explore more deeply the topic of a repeatable methodology, the first of the four components of a complete strategy execution program. We'll provide an overview of what such a methodology must contain, and why a methodology is so critical. Let's start with the basics.

A methodology, or method, is another name for any step-by-step approach to getting something done. We have methodologies all around us at work and at home, even though we may call them by different names. A recipe for baking a cake is really a methodology. The design and construction processes for building a house constitute a methodology. Most professions have a variety of standard practices to follow to arrive at long-term success. Software developers, architects, engineers, even physicians all have standard, repeatable practices they follow to complete their work successfully. These tried-and-true methods usually emerge as a result of best practices, standards, rules, and procedures developed over a number of years.

Just as the purpose of a home-construction methodology is to build excellent homes, the purpose of a *business-building* methodology is to build excellent businesses. In Chapter 6, we pointed out that customer excellence caters to the end-user or the customer. In the home-construction example, an excellent home caters to homeowners' preferences, including style, comfort, energy efficiency, and price. Similarly, a business-building methodology caters to the goals of business owners: profitable and predictable growth, engaged employees, strong reputation, and a large and loyal customer base.

The *initial* success of a business depends primarily on the ability to build top quality products or services. An organization's *enduring* success depends on building the business itself, in addition to its products and services. Understanding this distinction is critical. You must use a methodology that's *designed* for whatever it is you're building if you expect to achieve consistent results.

A business-building methodology must include the steps that are essential for an organization to build and sustain a healthy, growing business. It must define how the organization sets it goals and priorities, and organizes its resources to best achieve those goals. It must teach the organization how to stay focused on what's important, while dealing with the inevitable surprises that occur regularly in life. It must provide ways to identify where the organization is on plan (or off), and do so in real-time.

Finally, and most importantly, a business-building methodology must provide a framework for an organization, itself, to learn and grow as its size and complexity grows—a way to increase its capability to learn and grow faster than its challenges. Successfully applying a sound business-building methodology increases the percentage of time that an organization spends in Quadrant II. Failure to do this leads to quickly drifting out of Quadrant II and, ultimately, back into Quadrant III.

Where do you find a business-building methodology? This was the question we asked ourselves as we began to tackle this issue. We found an abundance of business-building concepts and best practices by such thought leaders such as Michael Porter, Michael Gerber, Edwards Deming, Stephen Covey, David Allen, Peter Senge, Peter Drucker, Robert Kaplan, David Norton, Jim Collins, Ram Charan, and so on. But even with this wealth of ideas, we discovered a bigger problem: we couldn't identify a single integrated business-building methodology that was practical for small and midsized businesses.

In other words, we were able to find integrated, well-defined instructions for designing and building a house, but we couldn't find a detailed methodology for designing and building a *business* that builds houses (or for that matter, any kind of business). This revelation gave us additional insight into why organizations face such tremendous execution challenges. Michael Gerber made a similar point in his book *The E-Myth Revisited*. He points out that we can learn a lot from the franchise world. Franchisors realize they're selling two products: the end customer's product *and* a business model for making money delivering such services. McDonalds, for example, sells more than just hamburgers. They're also selling speed, lower prices, and fun, as in fun food.

As a result, we at Six Disciplines reviewed many best practices and developed a business-building methodology, which is detailed in my book, *Six Disciplines for Excellence*. Our research identified six fundamental disciplines that need to be incorporated into a single, repeatable methodology. These disciplines include setting strategy, developing plans, organizing and aligning resources, managing execution, enabling innovation, and encouraging organizational learning. Each of these six disciplines is further broken down into four to six detailed steps that prescribe how to perform each discipline. The resulting methodology involves six disciplines and thirty-one steps, which are depicted in Figure 7.0.

You can attempt to find or build your own methodology, if you want to invest the time and effort to do so. And, we're not saying that our methodology is the *only* way to attack this challenge. We *are* absolutely advocating this: *every organization that is serious about excellence and execution **must** practice some defined methodology as the foundation of its efforts.*

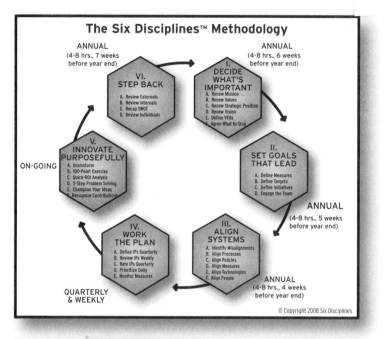

Figure 7.0–The Six Disciplines Methodology: six disciplines, thirty-one steps, in a single, repeatable methodology

The assumption in *having* a methodology is that it is used repeatedly. Repeatability is a topic worth looking at in more detail.

Repeatability is critical to learning. For example, how good were you the first time you rode a bike, pitched a ball, or gave a speech? Individuals learn by doing, and organizations must do the same thing. As in all types of endeavors, it takes practice and repetition to become excellent. The absolute foundation of building an organization that is increasing its ability to execute is a *repeatable* methodology.

You can think of the six disciplines in our methodology as a series of cycles: annually, quarterly, weekly and daily. With each successive pass, they help grow your organization's ability to deal with an ever-changing and increasingly challenging business environment.

These six fundamental disciplines distill and integrate into one cohesive whole many of the separate best practices discussed earlier, from the areas of strategic planning, continuous improvement, organizational learning, business process automation, performance management, and quality management.

Along the way, we stripped out concepts and processes that don't apply to small or midsized businesses, and we've peppered this synergistic mix with time-tested principles and empowering tools to offer the best of the best. Thousands of hours of market and field research, and more than 100 man-years of trial and error are the foundation of this business-building methodology, giving it a unified, experience-based quality.

The result is a repeatable organizational learning model. We believe that the necessity for repeatability is what business people inherently understand when they define excellence as an enduring pursuit—an on-going journey that never ends. We're building on that truth and challenging business leaders to realize that an enduring pursuit requires an enduring approach. Since today's success will stimulate future growth and change, tomorrow's challenges will not only be *different*, they'll be *bigger*. This means organizations must *learn how to learn* so that they are always preparing for tomorrow. Otherwise, growth and success will lead to challenges that overwhelm their ability to execute strategy.

Let's move on to another topic related to learning: team member engagement. You've probably heard the old joke in which someone asks a CEO how many people work in his company and he responds, "About half of them." This isn't funny when you look at the following statistics, and begin to realize how much time, energy, and resources are wasted every day. An important goal for any business-building methodology is to address how to *engage the team.*

According to research from The Gallup Organization, regarding the U.S. working population, 26 percent are engaged, 55 percent are not engaged, and 19 percent are actively disengaged. The most engaged workplaces (those in the top 25 percent of Q12 scores,) were:

- 50 percent more likely to have lower turnover
- 56 percent more likely to have higher-than-average customer loyalty
- 38 percent more likely to have above-average productivity
- and 27 percent more likely to report higher profitability[1]

From a poll of 23,000 employees cited in Dr. Stephen Covey's, *The 8th Habit*:

- Only 37 percent said they have a clear understanding of what their organization is trying to achieve and why
- Only 20 percent were enthusiastic about their team's and their organization's goals, said they have a clear link between their tasks and their team's organizational goals, and fully trusted the organization they worked for
- Only 15 percent felt that their organization fully enables them to execute key goals [2]

It's the realities these statistics represent that have caused us to place such a high priority on communication and engagement while designing the methodology and the complete program for implementing it.

Another priority of the methodology is to connect long-term goals with daily decisions. To do this requires connecting people's activities to the company's strategy—from the top to the bottom of the organization. It requires a clear process for defining strategy and goals that are then translated into team and individual goals. Similar to assembling a symphony orchestra, something that requires music, a conductor, instruments, expert musicians, and lots of practice, the process of aligning everyone's priorities is a skill that an organization must learn in order to be successful.

All the strategy, planning, goal setting, alignment and prioritization eventually comes down to choosing what action to take—what you're doing at this instant, as illustrated in Figure 7.1. The daily question to ask yourself is this: "*Are the activities you're working on aligned with what's important to the company?*"

Another benefit of having a repeatable and *documented* business-building methodology is the *accumulation* of knowledge by individuals and teams. Defining a process and then documenting changes to that process reinforces the learning that occurs so that you don't forget it. When many individuals use a common methodology, the rate of accumulated learning that is shared is accelerated. As in the construction industry, with its documented standards accumulated from many generations of building experience, a shared language and approach promotes effective communication and shared learning.

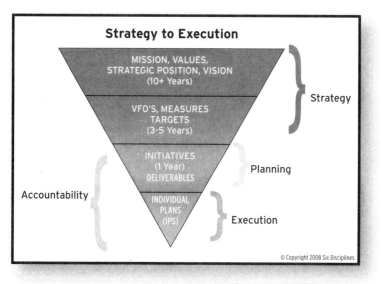

Figure 7.1–Strategy to execution: the translation of organizational strategy to the daily tasks of individuals.

Accumulating business-building knowledge enables faster transfer to others. This is particularly critical in growing organizations that are increasing in complexity faster than they are increasing in size. Recall previously that doubling the number of employees results in a four-fold increase in communications complexity. If that weren't enough, a growing business also faces larger competitors, plus ever-changing external business conditions such as technology, economics, regulations, and so on. And finally, hiring new employees who don't understand the business can increase the turnover of experienced workers. A tremendous value of a repeatable methodology is that it improves the effort to integrate increasingly larger team members into the organization. How? By helping individuals focus on what to do and by helping teams learn to work together and transfer knowledge more effectively.

Using a defined methodology also enables individuals within the organization to identify the root causes of quality variation, and eliminate them. For example, a detailed checklist of all the necessary steps to be performed for any given process reduces the likelihood that one of the steps will be missed. In addition, if quality varies unacceptably, the actual steps completed can be compared to the steps listed in the process to eliminate process errors as a possible cause. Imagine the flight checklist that every pilot goes through before every flight. Even though the pilot is experienced, it's not wise to depend on memory to deliver excellence.

[SUMMARY]

- The goal of a complete strategy execution program is to enable organizations to spend an increasing amount of time in Quadrant II. Here, their performance is more predictable and sustainable, and execution of strategy becomes balanced.
- Achieving this goal requires thinking *holistically* about the business—how to make all components, people, processes, policies, key measures, assets and strategies work together to meet the promises made to customers and other stakeholders and to repeat these in a predictable fashion.
- Be aware that reading about each discipline separately doesn't make your business perform better instantly any more than taking five golf lessons makes you a good golfer. In the end, you have to learn how to *use* all of the disciplines *together,* and the only way to truly learn them is by doing.
- In addition, the disciplines must be used in conjunction with the other three required elements of a complete strategy

execution program: accountability coaching, an execution system, and the benefits of community learning.

There you have it: the first requirement of a *complete program for strategy execution*. Practicing a business-building methodology consistently is not easy. In fact, it's so difficult that most organizations can't make it stick without assistance. It takes someone outside the organization who is trained to guide you from where you are today to where you want to be tomorrow. That's why you need the second element of the program: an accountability coach. This individual and the importance of their role is described in Chapter 8.

[Accountability Coaching]

" An essential tool for sustaining a successful strategy execution program is accountability coaching from outside the organization.*"*

Of all the topics in this book, *accountability coaching* offers the most insight into what it takes to deliver a complete strategy execution program. Most leaders fail to understand the implications of the human nature barriers we discussed earlier, and coaching directly addresses these barriers.

Our natural tendency is to do what we like doing, not necessarily what we should. For example, we interact every day with business leaders who love talking about their vision and what their business could become. But they don't like taking the time to plan the steps for getting there. These leaders typically don't follow up with their employees to make sure they're addressing and resolving the many issues that *always* come up on the way to getting "there." A company may start in Quadrant I and weave its way into Quadrant IV for a while, but as an organization, doing what it likes instead of what needs to be done eventually lands it in Quadrant III.

We find most business leaders recognize this tendency in themselves, but they often fail to recognize that it exists in *everyone else* within the organization as well. Any complete strategy execution program must address this tendency or, otherwise, yield to unpredictability and mediocrity.

The First Complete Strategy Execution Program

VI.
STEP
BACK
Learn

I.
DECIDE
WHAT'S
IMPORTANT
Strategy

II.
SET GOALS
THAT LEAD
Plan

III.
ALIGN
SYSTEMS
Organize

IV.
WORK
THE PLAN
Execute

V.
INNOVATE
PURPOSEFULLY
Innovate

• Repeatable Methodology
• **Accountability Coaching**
• Execution System
• Community Learning

© Copyright 2008 Six Disciplines

Renowned business leaders have developed a variety of approaches to address these human nature issues, from carrot-and-stick incentives, to even more extreme measures. Jack Welch transformed General Electric into one of the highest performing organizations in the world with an extraordinarily clear set of accountability rules for his top leaders. For simplicity, I'll paraphrase Welch's approach: If your business unit is not in the top two of your industry market share, you will be replaced, or your unit will be sold. This drastic approach earned him the nickname Neutron Jack. Other leaders have encouraged performance using other extreme motivators such as enormous profit sharing, market gain sharing, or stock options.

Extending the principles of coaching, we've found success is enhanced through accountability coaching—not just for the executives, but for the entire organization. Accountability means being answerable to someone. It's been my experience that just a little bit of "answerability" on a regular basis can make a huge difference in whether people maintain their focus on their priorities.

One example of accountability that may sound silly is found in my home office—but the point being made is anything but trivial. When we sold Solomon Software, my wife Rhonda and I decided to build a personal office onto our home to accommodate my business meetings. We hired a woman named Lori to keep this high traffic area clean. Every other Tuesday she comes to take care of my office. And guess what I'm doing the night before? Yes, I'm opening mail, filing, putting away open books and papers strewn all over. If Lori postpones cleaning for some reason, I don't do a thing that week. Basically I'm getting two values from Lori's service. My office is getting cleaned *and* she's providing a sense of accountability that helps me stay on top of the mail and clutter.

From our fieldwork, we're learning that an essential tool for sustaining a successful strategy execution program is accountability coaching from *outside* the organization. Someone who is not part of your organization can bring a nonbiased perspective that's not tainted by being part of the organization. This requires that your organization finds a trusted outside advisor, and give that advisor permission to understand your company and its priorities, in order to continue making sure these priorities are pursued.

The accountability that coaching provides is not a panacea. Many different things get us off track, and different approaches are required for different people. Sometimes different approaches are needed for the same person at different times depending on what is at hand. Accountability coaching is just one of the four required components that all work together to help an organization sustain a successful strategy execution program.

Unfortunately, many people view accountability as something negative. They think accountability is something that is held against them when things go wrong, or when performance doesn't meet expectations. Much of this expectation comes from the one-sided association of accountability with finger pointing and blaming others.

To execute strategy more effectively, a more positive and useful definition of accountability is required. We need to view accountability as both an organizational mindset *and* a series of behaviors, both of which we can learn and improve upon over time. We need to develop this mindset and ingrain it in our employees so that it becomes part of our organization's cultural DNA. As you'll soon see, this is where accountability coaching and community learning (Chapter 10) integrate in a new and powerful way.

Accountability requires a level of self-leadership that includes making, keeping, and answering for personal commitments. Such a perspective focuses on both current and future efforts as opposed to reactive excuses which are a veiled way of saying, "I'm not good enough to manage this." Using this more positive definition of accountability, we can move to a new level of doing everything possible within our capabilities to overcome ever-increasing challenges.

The premise regarding accountability behind our coaching model has been validated in dozens of organizations.[1] This accountability model asserts that most employees in organizations will learn to be accountable—that is, they'll do what is needed and expected—proportionate to the extent in which three factors are present:

- Expectations are clear
- These expectation are perceived as credible and reasonable because the employees were involved in setting them
- Employees understand the impact of success, or lack thereof, on the organization

When these three factors aren't in place, employees can't achieve their potential, no matter what kind of people they are.

A critical element for creating company-wide accountability is to put appropriate focus on results, not activities. For most employees, it's more motivating to be told what needs to be done and why, but not how. We're not suggesting that the activities to get results should be ignored. In fact, we believe aligning daily activities (how employees spend their time) is so critical that we've devoted an entire chapter of this book (Chapter 9) to exploring its importance.

The bottom line is this: being accountable to ourselves is not enough. We clearly need others, preferably outside of our organization, to hold us accountable and to help us accelerate our learning. We need others to help us fight the continual battles against our own human nature and our tendency to do what we want to do, rather than what we need to do. We need others to challenge our way of thinking and acting. We need others to help us increase our capability to manage the next challenge. We need others to learn how to do this faster than we can do it on our own. Finally, we need others to help make change last within our organizations, to make the new way of working "stick." That's what accountability coaching is all about.

Let's take a more in-depth look at the benefits of coaching in general, and specifically what led us to include accountability coaching as one of the four major tenets of the first complete strategy execution program, specifically for small and mid-sized businesses.

In deciding what coaching is, the International Coaching Federation (ICF) casts the widest net with its definition:

> "ICF defines coaching as partnering with clients in a thought-provoking and creative pro-cess that inspires them to maximize their personal

and professional potential. Individuals who engage in a coaching relationship can expect to experience fresh perspectives on personal challenges and opportunities, enhanced thinking and decision making skills, enhanced interpersonal effectiveness, and increased confidence in carrying out their chosen work and life roles."[2]

We want to further clarify what accountability coaching is and is not:

Accountability Coaching is Methodology-focused

Accountability coaches are seasoned business executives who guide organizations through the use of the repeatable business-building methodology. They help organizations figure out where to start and what to work on, in what order, to improve their business-building capability. They leverage their learning from other accountability coaches and clients in the application of the methodology to a specific situation.

Accountability Coaching is Enduring

Through a planned series of quarterly and annual face-to-face meetings (as well as daily and weekly contact), accountability coaching monitors and measures progress, enabling companies to make mid-course corrections. It's a never-ending process that leverages last quarter's and last year's lessons to move to help organizations achieve higher performance levels in the future.

Accountability Coaching is Not Therapy

A therapist is useful in healing the wounds and problems of the past; accountability coaching is about helping already healthy individuals and organizations with the challenges of the present, and assisting them in moving forward.

Accountability Coaching is Not Consulting

Consultants are more project-focused than accountability coaches. They're often brought in to identify problems and to offer suggestions for the solution, but they're typically not involved as a long-term stakeholder in the results of the solution. Accountability coaches don't just point out problems or offer suggestions. Organizations don't need more advice or more ivory tower theory. They want—*need* results. Accountability coaches use a hands-on approach to help the leadership team examine stakeholder feedback and set strategy. They then work with teams and individuals to build more detailed quarterly operating plans and organize resources to meet those plans. Finally, every individual in the organization uses the execution system (see the next chapter) to track his or her own progress and to proactively manage any day-to-day surprises. Instead of *telling* companies what to do, accountability coaches *show* how individuals need to provide self leadership for their plans. In other words, accountability coaches are engaged as an external catalyst for stimulating the execution capability of organizations.

"Coaching simply speeds up a process of change that would most likely occur anyway if an individual had enough time. Without a coaching program that forces a client to focus and make time, people sometimes miss the real issues they need to focus on."[3]

Accountability coaching draws its influences from the successes of a narrower niche, executive coaching. Although a different type of coaching, it provides useful insight into accountability coaching as well. In 2004, a *Harvard Business Review* report summarized the following key reasons why executive coaching works:

- Coaching engages with employees in customized ways that acknowledge and honor their individuality.
- The essentially human nature of coaching is what makes it work, and also what makes it nearly impossible to quantify.
- In most organizations, lasting change usually occurs slowly, one person at a time, gaining momentum as more workers buy in.
- To accelerate change and make it stick, they recommend systematically coordinating one-on-one coaching interventions that serve a larger objective.
- Once senior leaders have changed their behavior, it's easier for them to influence subordinates to do the same. [4]

Total Organizational Engagement

One of the early findings in our research was that the typical organization's leadership team engaged very rapidly around the concept of a strategy execution program for planning and executing better. They quickly embraced both the purpose and the methodology. What we didn't find, however, was engagement by employees further down in the organization. In fact, the further down in organization, the less engagement there was. By total organizational engagement we mean that employees across the *entire company* learn to understand the importance of the business-building program for the company's future, and for their own work effectiveness.

The more we evaluated what was happening, the more we uncovered a fundamental principle: for individuals to really embrace the strategy execution program (including the technology of an execution system, which we will discuss in Chapter 9), the program had to connect each team member to the company strategy, as well as help *every individual* do his or her job better. A generic instruction, "Do this because it will benefit the organization as a whole" is not enough of a motivator. The program, and the message about the program, must deliver personalized benefit to each individual.

Backing up for a second, the reason this concept was adopted so quickly at the company leadership level was because it helped them do their job of formulating strategy and plans, and managing their execution. What is needed is a repeatable method to engage the entire workforce, enabling them to realize how this program was going to actually make *their* roles, *their* jobs, perhaps even *their* lives—easier. We're now able to break through this important barrier.

We've learned that capturing the hearts of individual workers is a continuous journey that starts at the top of the organization and works its way throughout the company. An enduring approach to employee engagement begins with the company leadership team and is facilitated continuously by accountability coaching at succeeding levels in the organization.

There are a number of requirements that serve as the foundation for total organizational engagement. Most leaders understand by now that plastering the walls with motivational posters will not change employee attitudes, nor will it improve employee engagement. Improving employee engagement calls for specifying and rewarding the desired behaviors—not just the desired attitudes.

As we came to grips with these truths, we modified our methodology and the accountability coaching model to deliver additional value and engagement at *all* levels of the organization. Figure 8.0 shows how the total organizational engagement model works.

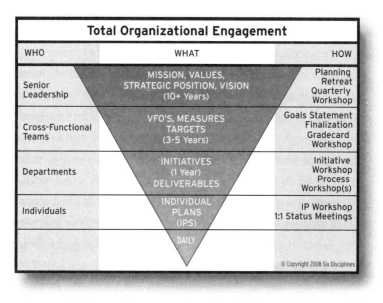

Total Organizational Engagement		
WHO	WHAT	HOW
Senior Leadership	MISSION, VALUES, STRATEGIC POSITION, VISION (10+ Years)	Planning Retreat Quarterly Workshop
Cross-Functional Teams	VFO'S, MEASURES TARGETS (3-5 Years)	Goals Statement Finalization Gradecard Workshop
Departments	INITIATIVES (1 Year) DELIVERABLES	Initiative Workshop Process Workshop(s)
Individuals	INDIVIDUAL PLANS (IPS)	IP Workshop 1:1 Status Meetings
	DAILY	

© Copyright 2008 Six Disciplines

Figure 8.0–A model for total organizational engagement

The total organizational engagement model above depends on a complete strategy execution program—the combination of a repeatable business-building methodology, accountability coaching, an execution system, and community learning. The role of the accountability coach is to guide organizations through this model, and to drive the application and adoption of the principles to more employees in the organization, and to greater levels of usage by each person. In other words, total organizational engagement is measured in terms of both breadth and depth. It's a process that never ends, because as employees learn the principles, their capacity to do more increases. Generally speaking, successful execution of strategy today will lead to a larger workforce, bigger competitors, and better opportunities tomorrow. Growth must continue at least as fast as the pace of its challenges, or the organization will stagnate.

Notice the inverted triangle in Figure 8.0 that represents the *what*—the core business-building disciplines described in the methodology. These disciplines start by having senior leadership answering key strategic questions about mission, value, strategic position, and vision. At each successive layer in the diagram, plans become more short-term and more detailed, and eventually lead to the daily activities at the bottom. This represents what every employee is doing *today*—in real-time. In a perfectly aligned organization, all of these items would fit together with no wasted energy or effort. This ideal represents the ongoing journey that we call the pursuit of business excellence. Although we never perfectly achieve it, the focus on doing so improves our results.

The left side of Figure 8.0 shows the *who*—the different levels and types of workers, whose different needs must be addressed. Senior leadership is responsible for setting strategy and operating goals, and the cross-functional teams are responsible for defining and implementing the strategic change initiatives that move the organization from the status quo to where it needs to be. The departments are responsible for building best practice processes and the organizational expertise for executing those processes. And last (but certainly not least) is the individual worker, who needs a personalized view of priorities that represent slices of corporate initiatives and department initiatives. Accountability coaches must understand the difference in these organizational levels and how they interact with each other. The challenge is that it changes from organization to organization—and even within an organization, as it grows and matures.

The right side of Figure 8.0 shows the *how*—a planned and ongoing series of on-the-job workshops that help employees at every level of the organization learn how to apply the business-building methodology to their particular role or function. The fundamental principle here is that the individual and the company start from wherever they are, and then build from there by doing. As in music, sports, or any area, learning is staged according to ability. All future learning is built upon the past, and a compounding of learning occurs. (There's much more about the power of synergy of all the pieces working together in the final two chapters of this book.)

The role of the accountability coach is to understand this process and guide the organization through it. The coach reminds you of the commitments you've made to yourself and your organization, so that these efforts don't get swallowed up by the day-to-day fray of business life.

The end result is that your organization establishes a regular rhythm (described in Chapter 7, and shown in Figure 8.1) where annual examinations of strategy and organizational performance occur, followed by annual and quarterly planning at the corporate, initiative, and individual level. Monthly, weekly, and even daily disciplines are developed that help each employee continue learning how to make better decisions and align his or her activities with company goals. In other words, your organization is continually *learning how to learn*.

From our field research, we learned what it takes to be an effective accountability coach. And we have good news for the over-forty crowd. At least one of the members of the accountability coaching team needs to be a seasoned executive. He

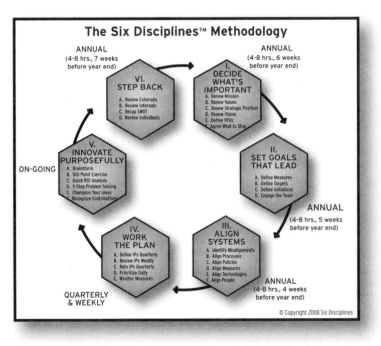

Figure 8.1–The *rhythm* of a repeatable business-building methodology

or she must have walked in the shoes of a CEO of a small or midsized business. This coach must be able to communicate peer-to-peer with other CEOs. He or she must have the seasoning that twenty-five to thirty years of experience provides and the perspective that understands the difference between quick fixes and enduring approaches. This coach needs to have experienced growth or have worked in different size organizations to understand how the dynamics of size affects operations and execution. He or she needs to have the highest standards of integrity to build a long-term, trusted relationship with client organizations. Finally, an accountability coach needs to be truly motivated to pass on what he or she has already learned to the next generation of business leaders. And, this rare individual must have a sense of calling to perform this work well.

In the broadest sense, an accountability coach is an agent of change. Kurt Lewin, considered to be the founder of modern social psychology and a change management expert, provides a relevant roadmap of the organizational change process for companies that enroll in such a company-wide strategy execution program. According to Lewin, implementing organizational change is a three-step process of *unfreezing, changing,* and *refreezing.* *Unfreezing* is the most important step. Deciding to adopt a new approach to executing strategy, as outlined in this book, is a major change. Unfreezing involves preparing individuals within the organization for the changes to come. Unfreezing is the step that helps employees accept and support the upcoming changes within their organization. To get the workforce to buy into and support change, the accountability coach must work closely in conjunction with the CEO. This is not accomplished in a single meeting, but by a series of collaborative meetings with senior leadership, by continual communication, and by on-going accountability coaching, eventually with the entire workforce on related topics.

This unfreezing process needs to take place before the new approach of executing strategy is implemented so the entire workforce is ready, open, and supportive. Unfortunately, this is the step that is usually ignored or insufficiently completed. When this happens, lasting change and the pursuit of enduring business excellence is always compromised.

Once the new approach to executing strategy is introduced, what becomes forefront is learning by doing to adopt a new, more effective way of working. It takes time to absorb, adopt, and embrace a new way of working. Sometimes it takes a number of quarters, or even years. Therein lies the major shortcoming of most business improvement programs. They don't seem to be embraced long enough to take hold within the organization. It's not that the programs are inadequate from a content perspective. What happens is the organization isn't held accountable by anyone for continuing to use it long enough to produce enduring results.

As frequently stated, excellence is an enduring pursuit; it requires an enduring approach. By enduring, we mean that the program grows with the business, year after year. An enduring program encourages every employee to fight against the distractions, to align their plans and activities every day to support the organization's strategies in order to achieve its goals. Over time, the practice of activity alignment (supported by accountability coaching) becomes an individual and organizational habit, increasing the company's ability to continually learn and improve performance.

Finally, change management expert Lewin suggests that a *refreezing* phase needs to take place, meaning a conscious plan for making the new way of working permanent. That's where an external accountability coach makes all the difference. These coaches help you monitor and measure progress, and periodically check to ensure that the new way of executing strategy remains in place and that your organization has not drifted back to its old, ineffective ways of operating.

[SUMMARY]

- Any complete strategy execution program must address our tendency to do what we like to do, rather than do what we know we should. Accountability coaching is a key component of a complete program that directly addresses this tendency.
- A more positive and useful definition of accountability is needed in order for us to execute strategy more effectively.
- Accountability coaching is methodology-focused and enduring; it is not therapy or consulting.
- Total organizational engagement with the strategy execution program is necessary in order for the changes in work behavior to endure.
- A relevant roadmap of the organizational change process exists for companies that enroll in such a company-wide strategy execution program.

In the next chapter, we will present the behind-the-scenes role of technology, in the form of an execution system, to help every one of your team members to proactively align his or her daily activities to the priorities of your company.

CHAPTER 9

[An Execution System]

" Without an execution system, an organization becomes unpredictable at best and eventually declines in its ability to execute, especially as it grows. *"*

What Is an Execution System?

The execution system is the third element of the complete program. And as with all other elements it does not function alone. Its effectiveness depends upon the inter-workings of the other components.

The primary role of the *execution system* component is to help organizations get the right things done. To do this

requires identifying execution problems as early as possible and addressing them.

To explain this concept, I'm going to use a proven principle from the software industry that is broadly applicable when building any system. The principle is: the earlier you catch an error, the less costly it is to fix.

The study results shown in Figure 9.0 illustrates this principle.[1] In this research, it was found that on the average it costs 6.5 times as much to fix an error in software once it is coded, compared to correcting it during the requirements phase of a project. It cost fifteen times as much in the testing stage, and eighty times as much once the error is deployed. Actually, the cost to fix an error that is deployed can be orders of magnitude more expensive. Today there are software products that have millions and even hundreds of millions of users. The support costs of supporting, reporting, testing, deploying, and documenting grows geometrically with usage.

Think of an organization as a system for deciding what to do (a strategy, a plan) and then managing the execution of that plan. When the system (the business) makes an error, choosing to do the wrong thing or forgetting to do something that is required, the problem must be corrected. The longer it takes to detect the problem, the more it costs to fix. If the business has no system in place to set, manage, and monitor strategy execution, the process is not only error-prone, it's a huge disaster waiting to happen. Without such a system, an organization becomes unpredictable

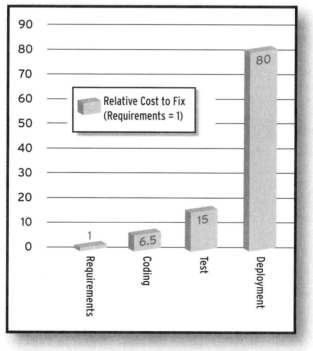

Figure 9.0–The relative cost to fix errors in software development

at best and eventually declines in its ability to execute, especially as it grows.

This is why it's important that an execution system enables an organization to focus on learning to identify execution problems as early as possible. Based on our experience, we have indentified five primary types of organizational errors that cause execution failures within an organization:

- **Change**—The requirements for what is to be delivered have changed. A common example that occurs in the sales world when first setting sales goals is to define a goal as *orders* as opposed to *contracts signed*. An order might be a verbal agreement, but the order can't be booked and shipped until a signed contract is in hand. This kind of confusion can create big misunderstandings in revenue recognition and cash flow for a business. In the construction world, a client change in the specifications can make a huge difference in cost, schedule, and profitability.

- **Clarity**—The requirements do not change but are misunderstood (not clear). The party specifying the requirements of a project assumes the party working on the project understands. (Oh, I thought patio doors swing open like my neighbors, not slide back and forth.) These are particularly difficult to spot until it's too late.

- **Dependency**—The outcome depended on some other result (or person's activities or deliverables) that did not get delivered on time. Learning to account for and manage external dependencies is an essential skill in proactive alignment.

- **Estimation**—Requirements are clear, but the estimate for completion is not correct. This could be due to many factors such as skill of implementer, poor design, unaccounted for risks, and so forth. In the sales world, this could be an error in the percentage of leads that can be closed.
- **Availability**—The expected number of resources assumed in the plan was not available. The reasons for this vary from unexpected sickness and reassignment to overruns on other projects and frequently, working on things that were not planned (crowding out room for those that were).

Remember: the Execution Revolution is about giving organizations the opportunity to attack the biggest problem in business in a new way. As we pursued this objective in our research, it became clear that wasted, misaligned resources are a huge part of the problem.

Successful companies grow and change, and, as a result, they add new talent to their workforces. Whatever the rate of growth in headcount, the growth in communication complexity is growing much faster (Figure 9.1). For example, a hundred-person organization is approximately thirty-three times the size of a three-person organization, but the communications possibilities are 1,650 times more complex!

We concluded that one of the pillars of any program designed to produce enduring results is a proactive execution system, one that helps its users *anticipate* potential misalignments and learn to spot or prevent them as early as possible. Consider the melting ice cube analogy. Each moment of the day, the employees in every organization have a multitude of things competing for

The Challenge of Communication			
# People	# Possible Different Interactions	Increase in People	Increase in Communications Complexity
3	3		
25	300	8x	100x
50	1,225	17x	408x
100	4,950	33x	1,650x
1,000	499,500	333x	166,500x

© Copyright 2008 Six Disciplines

Figure 9.1–The challenge of communication as headcount increases

their time and attention. Without a system that creates continuous focus on anticipating and preventing misalignments, the organization melts away: progress slows, and considerable time and money are wasted and frustrations increase.

We're not the first to observe this need for alignment tools. In Chapter 4, we reviewed a number of developments that have led to advancements and innovations in organizational alignment. It is because of progress in areas such as this that we have the pieces necessary to assemble a *complete* program.

Organizations operating in Quadrant I can benefit from tools such as the balanced scorecard for formulating and communicating a well-balanced strategy. This tool also helps business leaders communicate where they want to go, which leads to better-aligned plans.

For companies operating in Quadrant IV, there have been significant innovations in process automation. The purpose of a properly engineered process is to align all company activities so they can be executed predictably and efficiently. This is a form of proactive alignment. Other examples include advancements in performance management software, which connects divisions, departments, and teams to critical success metrics. These metrics also help individuals focus on doing the right things. Email calendaring also has the potential for aligning people around schedules. Email, in general, can be an alignment tool when it helps employees communicate clearly (but of course it frequently is not.)

What's most encouraging is that we seem to be on the verge of marrying some of these best practices into an integrated whole. The Quadrant IV tools such as word processing, ERP, spreadsheets, and email help us get things done better, faster, and cheaper. But for the most part, they do not really guide individual team members in determining whether what they are doing are the *right things to do*. It's easy to slip into "efficiency frenzy" at the expense of effectiveness. Our findings are that an execution system needs to include the following elements:

- Methodology automation
- Time management
- Real-time activity alignment
- Weekly external review cycle
- Total organizational engagement (enrollment)
- Execution measurement

Let's explore each of these key attributes of an execution system.

Methodology Automation

The business-building approach embodied in the repeatable methodology needs to be automated. This ensures that the development, communication, and management of strategy, plans and activities can be performed efficiently. Automation is especially needed to deal with the extensive travel, work-at-home, and virtual relationships that exist in today's organizations.

While the use of technology is a given, the focus on automation needs to expand. Beyond the implementation of specific best practices, such as creating a word document or spreadsheet, the attention needs to shift to integrating all components necessary for building solid plans and managing the daily execution of challenges. The key is shifting the emphasis to the *effectiveness* side of the decision-making equation, thereby bringing balance to the *efficiency* side, using innovations from the past twenty years. To remain longer in Quadrant II, an organization must develop the capability to balance effectiveness with efficiency. It must have both growth strategies in place *and* be able to execute them.

We're seeing more evidence of this trend toward methodology automation in the development of CRM, performance management and ERP systems. All of these tools are beginning to increase their functionality with goal-setting and measurement support, integration of scorecards, and knowledge management.

Time Management

" Time is the scarcest resource and unless it is managed, nothing else can be managed."

—Peter Drucker

In his classic book *The Effective Executive*, Peter Drucker discusses essential practices that are hallmarks of effective *executives*. The first of these practices is: *Effective executives know where their time goes.* Actually, this general principle can be extended to the entire workforce. Everyone in an organization needs to better understand how they're spending their time and learn to manage all time that is under their control.

We believe that time management by every person in the company is critical to proactively achieving alignment. More effective execution depends on everyone increasing their ability to do the right things and tracking time is fundamental to knowing whether you are (doing the right things). We also find that major failures to meeting plans fall into the five categories of execution errors described earlier: *change, clarity, dependency, estimation* and *availability.* To improve execution, we need to improve the learning rate for detecting or preventing these various problems.

It turns out that in four of five of these categories (except external *dependency*), time management accelerates identifying problems earlier. In the case of estimation errors, time management is directly related to improving skills in early problem identification.

Time management reveals misunderstandings much sooner so that they don't crop up when a project is delivered. Then, it's too late to do anything about the misunderstandings. There's also a compounding effect for not catching this problem in time. If twice the allotted time is spent on deliverable A, there's no longer enough time for deliverable B—and someone else is depending on deliverable B for deliverable C. The ripple effect of this variability creates the kind of unpredictable performance we frequently see in many companies.

Time management also helps reveal how a company is investing its money. We recently had a client who was evaluating whether it was investing enough to capture new clients. They did a very smart thing. They benchmarked the total sales and marketing expenses of a competitor and divided those expenses by the number of new customer adds. This gave them a multi-year trend on total cost of acquiring new customers. Comparing that number to their own number revealed that they were significantly under investing compared to their competitor.

In almost every business, the biggest single costs are the expenses related to the workforce: wages, benefits, insurance, incentives, workstations, training, and so on. If you don't build the discipline of time management into your organization so that everyone knows how they're spending their time, the learning that can promote better execution is significantly hampered.

Real-Time Activity Alignment

"The key is not to prioritize what's on your schedule,
but to schedule your priorities.**"**

—*Dr. Stephen Covey*

The next step in building an effective execution system is bringing together two different domains of expertise. For example, most office workers I know have a fairly email-centric desktop, with a few other applications open, depending on their role. In addition to email, a salesperson may have at their fingertips a contact management system, an order processing screen, and perhaps a spreadsheet with some forecast assumptions. In smaller organizations, salespeople may also be asked to participate in requirement reviews for new products, evaluate new marketing materials, and attend an evaluation of proposed changes to their sales management process. And, hopefully, they have some professional development goals and an annual review coming up.

Part of a team member achieving real-time activity alignment is sitting down periodically (we recommend quarterly) with his or her team leader and agreeing on what is the best use of that team member's time, given the company's goals. This agreement is a plan for the team member and provides a framework against which the team member can evaluate the inevitable demands of daily activities for time and attention. The possible responses to these demands are:

- It's in my plan, so I'll do it.
- It's not in my plan, so I won't do it (perhaps it can be scheduled later).
- It's not in my plan, but it's important, so I'll change the plan and do it.

At this juncture in our technologies, there needs to be a marriage of our inbox to our plans, in order to give us a simple framework for evaluating each request. If not managed, these interruptions can drive the life of the worker. And the *urgent* overcomes the *important*.

We're now seeing the beginnings of this thinking emerging in applications focused on a particular type of worker. For example, the standard email footprint today (e.g., Microsoft Outlook) provides an easy way to place email on a calendar, task, or contact list. Traditional transaction-oriented vendors like Microsoft, SAP, Salesforce.com, NetSuite and others are extending this idea to their products that are built around an email interface, so that the inbox and, for example, sales management are much more tightly integrated. Not surprisingly, successful software companies that have a rich history of managing transactions have much to offer the Execution Revolution, as a result of their expertise in mainstream transaction processing.

What these software vendors don't yet have as part of their current offerings is a model for building a company-wide strategic plan that can be segmented into operational plans down to the individual level. Other thought leaders have developed pieces of the planning solution with balanced scorecards and performance management systems, but their integration of these with a company's transaction systems is insufficient, or if sufficient, is very expensive since these are distinctly separate systems. This dilemma speaks to the barriers of expertise and economics that we discussed in Chapter 5.

At Six Disciplines, we believe the long-term direction is clear. All players in this broad market space will ultimately converge on providing solutions for real-time activity alignment.

As shown in Figure 9.2, the Execution Revolution combines a variety of proven best practices, innovations and advances from many diverse technology disciplines developed over the past several decades. We believe that strategy execution programs represent a new category within the business excellence industry.

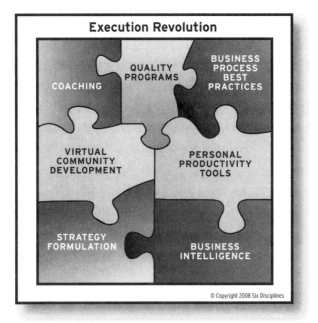

Figure 9.2–The convergence of best practices and innovations fueling the Execution Revolution

Advancements in this area are driving the Execution Revolution. We see evidence of this almost everywhere. ERP vendors have been broadening their application suites to cover more of the functions performed by an organization. And recently, the ERP market has seen a flurry of partnerships and acquisitions of business intelligence tools vendors. This consolidation is occurring because clients want their decision support capabilities tightly integrated with their day-to-day transaction data.

In addition, the performance management software industry is investing to more tightly integrate its products with the ERP vendors in order to bring their planning tools deeper into the organization and reach more of the workforce.

Today, CRM vendors are either combining with ERP vendors or are attempting to expand their products beyond the traditional CRM transaction set. Document management capabilities are also being more tightly integrated with work-flow solutions, and workflow solutions are being more tightly integrated into CRM solutions.

I could go on about how email, OLAP, dashboards, balanced scorecards, and so on, are all part of this giant convergence. My point, though, is this convergence is clearly underway and will continue for decades until its resulting products and ser-vices are easy and economical for the majority of the business market to use.

The area that seems to be lacking in this convergence, how-ever, is the integration of a business-building methodology, as described in Chapter 7. This element is critical, for without it, small and midsized businesses cannot systematically and pro-actively manage day-to-day activities by aligning them with organizational priorities. The main reason for the lack in this area is most of the advances in business tools are about doing things faster or cheaper, without bringing together the worlds of strategy and execution. A simple example of this problem today is email. It brings a world of communication to your desktop, but doesn't help you decide *which* items to act on—or *why*.

This hasn't been solved historically because to solve it at the individual level requires *every* team member *every* day to have a direct understanding of how a company's strategy drives his or her priorities. And it requires that the daily flow of activity requests be filtered through these priorities. This is a need whose time is right, and the pieces are finally falling into place to make the solution practical.

Weekly External Review Cycle

On a separate topic, a core part of becoming more proactive in organization alignment is creating a culture where everyone is accountable to regularly review their progress for the past week and plans for the next week with their team leader. What we learned is that a fifteen-to-thirty minute status review meeting once a week works better than a one-hour status meeting every other week. This kind of meeting creates a "synch point" between the team member and team leader. It forces team members to get out of the details once a week for a few minutes and declare whether anything is at risk in their plan.

Technology can help make this weekly review cycle as painless as possible. In our methodology, we use software to build an individual's plan on a quarterly basis. The integration between activity management and time management is tight. Once an individual's plan is built, it takes less than 10 minutes to prepare a brief weekly status that is then automatically emailed to the team leader.

This status report, however, doesn't replace the need for a one-on-one (face-to-face, if possible) meeting each week. Our experience shows that face-to-face meetings uncover misalignments *earlier* than if no meeting occurs at all. We believe the reason is humans communicate face-to-face more effectively than any other way. So a team member showing up for a meeting holds both the team member and team leader accountable for doing something they know they should do. This technique directly addresses the human nature hurdles we described in Chapter 5.

The approach for status reporting varies from organization to organization. Some prefer to complete these weekly meetings in team or department settings, while others prefer individual meetings. Some who have remote employees complete them by phone and webcam. Regardless of approach, these status meetings are a significant step in the right direction as far as proactively spotting execution issues—and correcting them quickly.

Total Organizational Engagement

I want to reiterate that involving the entire workforce in the strategy execution program accelerates organizational learning. I remember in the late 1980s, when Solomon Software first explored implementing email (yes, I am that old). We set up a pilot program in which a small group of employees were placed on the system. This experience taught me one big lesson in a hurry. Either *everyone* should be on the system—or no one should be on it at all. It was extremely frustrating to craft an email message for a group of four people and find out that one of the four individuals I wanted to send it to wasn't even on the email system. What to do? Email the message to three people, but print and send it to the fourth? Yuck!

The same dynamic is in play with an organization that's serious about sustaining its efforts to become better at executing strategy. It's much easier if everyone is using the system. Employees can communicate more effectively using the same terminology and technology. The shared learning occurs faster because the community is larger. And all areas of the company are brought under the same program. *Everyone is engaged in understanding company priorities and learning to more effectively align their daily activities.*

Execution Measurement

*"*If you can't measure it, you can't manage it.*"*

The keys to every profession typically consist of a few primary metrics that drive that organization. For consulting organizations, it might be consultant *utilization* or *realization*. For manufacturing companies, it might be defects or scrap. For software firms, it might be the number of new clients or licenses or average on-going revenue per client. In order for an organization to actually see the power of improving its ability to execute strategy, it *must* be able to measure this ability.

So how does a company measure its ability to execute strategy? An investor measures it by earnings growth and by the volatility of those earnings. Those are certainly good *lagging* measures. However, we've found that organizational learning occurs faster when *leading* measures are used.

For example, we recommend as part of the individual quarterly planning process that every team member rate whether his or her deliverables were met or not, and, if not, to explain the reason, using one of the five types of execution errors discussed earlier. We also recommend that each team member track the percent of deliverables completed on time.

This approach allows individuals, departments, and the company leadership to understand what barriers interfere with execution, and what to work on next. In addition, we recommend using what we call a "going-to-the-gym" measure. This measure tracks how well the organization is adhering to the basic discipline of preparing weekly status reports and conducting one-on-one meetings. The activities in this measure don't tell you how well you're executing, but they do indicate whether you're doing the things necessary to learn *how* to execute more effectively.

Please understand, we're not just talking about projects. We're talking about sales goals, customer satisfaction goals, budget goals—whatever is critical to the success of a given job and to the organization as a whole. Initially, this may sound overwhelming, but by using a well-defined methodology that is adopted and embraced by the entire company, and using the latest technology, this kind of strategy execution program inevitably becomes mainstream and very practical for small and midsized businesses.

Other useful measures we recommend to be tracked are ones addressing how well the company is meeting its strategic goals: sales, profitability, client acquisitions, and so on. We also recommend asking senior leadership to rate their plan achievement and progress toward their ten-year vision. Finally, we recommend that all stakeholders rate the company's performance relative to practicing the fundamental business-building disciplines described in the methodology. This entire measurement system is very similar to the approach used in the Malcolm Baldrige Quality Program survey, which is the cornerstone of the Baldrige evaluation of an organization's progress on its internal quality program.

The purpose behind the Execution Revolution is to create a systematic way for individuals and organizations to combat distractions and get aligned with what's important to the company's success. Unfortunately, all of us are barraged by interruptions and conflicting requests. Research from Gloria Marks shows that *the average worker is interrupted every eleven minutes on the job.*[2] Furthermore, her studies reveal that it takes those same workers about twenty-five minutes on average to return to the original task. Given a typical workday, this extrapolates to forty-four potential interruptions a day, and only nineteen opportunities to return to the original task or activity per day.

A 2007 Center for Creative Leadership's study of senior executives reports they are interrupted about every 30 to 40 minutes, leading to approximately 14 interruptions per day.[3] Researchers from Paisley and Glasgow Universities found that *typical office workers were checking for new email messages as often as thirty to forty times an hour,* affecting productivity levels and increasing pressure on the entire staff.[4] The Mesmo Consultancy recently claimed that over half of business email users were "self-inflicted emailaholics."[5] Their study indicated that *over 80 percent read every single email in their inbox.* What we need is a practical and systematic way to reduce distractions, stay focused, and continually align our daily activities to the priorities of the organization. That is exactly what an execution system used in context of a complete strategy execution program enables us to do.

[SUMMARY]

■ An execution system enables an organization to focus on learning to identify execution problems as early as possible.

■ There are five primary types of organizational errors or causes for execution failure within an organization: change, clarity, dependency, estimation and availability.

An execution system needs to include the following elements: methodology automation, time management, real-time activity alignment, weekly external review cycle, total organizational engagement, and execution measurement.

We have now described the third component of our complete program. Without it, we don't believe a strategy execution is sustainable, and certainly an organization will not reach its potential. The final element in our program is the role and impact of community learning. Chapter 10 explains why both elements (community and learning) are critical in overcoming the economic and expertise hurdles that are so difficult for small and midsized businesses.

[Community Learning]

" Think of these strategic
management best practices
as a core competency for an
organization. These practices
can be identified, codified,
and thus **shared with others,**
helping to move strategic
management from an art to a
science.'**"**

A complete strategy execution program depends upon the power of *community learning.* This final element helps provide the breadth and depth of expertise small and midsized organizations simply do not have. Communities also provide a powerful anecdote for our tendency to not do the things we know we should.

These two powerful ideas—*community* and *learning*— have a high degree of synergy. Both are necessary to a strategy

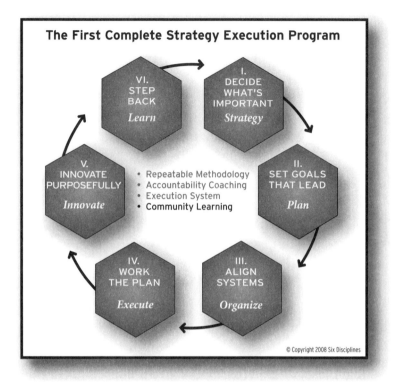

The First Complete Strategy Execution Program

VI.
STEP
BACK
Learn

I.
DECIDE
WHAT'S
IMPORTANT
Strategy

V.
INNOVATE
PURPOSEFULLY
Innovate

- Repeatable Methodology
- Accountability Coaching
- Execution System
- **Community Learning**

II.
SET GOALS
THAT LEAD
Plan

IV.
WORK
THE PLAN
Execute

III.
ALIGN
SYSTEMS
Organize

© Copyright 2008 Six Disciplines

execution program. First, the power of *community* is required to change the economics for implementing such a program within small and midsized organizations. Second, *learning* is required to overcome the natural tendency of individuals and organizations to wander from the very disciplines that can deliver them from the status quo.

Let's first understand more about the influence and impact of communities and how they facilitate learning. Dictionary.com defines community as: *"a group sharing common characteristics or interests and perceived or perceiving itself as distinct in some respect from the larger society within which it exists."*

The Execution Revolution for small and midsized businesses will be built around communities that share the following characteristics:

- A belief that their ultimate core competence is the ability to execute their strategy
- Use of a shared repeatable methodology that helps them organize their efforts so they can learn to execute better and speak the same language
- Accountability coaches who are experts in the same repeatable methodology they share
- The daily use of shared technology to integrate planning and activity alignment throughout the organization

It's a tall order to build a community that agrees to share these attributes. But the payback is significant in terms of the ability to leapfrog past the piecemeal approaches used in much larger companies. Even though it's difficult, it's worth the effort, because well-formed communities accelerate learning. In this sense, communities are a means to an end, namely, *learning*.

In the past four chapters, we've touched on powerful elements of community learning without pointing it out specifically. Let's walk through all the ways that community is part of a complete strategy execution program. Figure 10.0 shows a diagram of how these communities interact.

The next part of this chapter describes these emerging communities in *the order* that they are developing.

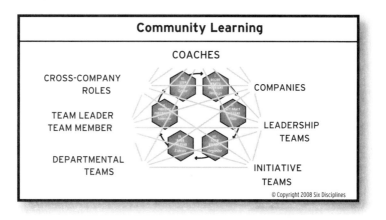

Figure 10.0–Learning among communities that practice the strategy execution program

The Coach Community

Coaches who are trained in a complete strategy execution program (the Six Disciplines methodology, for example) form their own community. They have a passion for sharing what they've learned with others. They share a desire to help businesses succeed. They share the experience of implementing a common business-building methodology across multiple businesses, helping these organizations learn faster about what works and what does not. The shared learning of the coaches benefits their clients since the best coaching practices learned from actual implementations are immediately transmitted to other clients.

As we discussed, the alternatives to coaching, activities such as reading books, attending seminars, and hiring consultants, produce fleeting results, at best. The accountability coaching community is essential to overcoming the barriers of inadequate expertise and our sometimes weak human nature. We all need encouragement and accountability to stay on the right path. The strength of the strategy execution program is built upon the strength of its coaching community.

The Leadership Team Community

It may at first appear that we're splitting hairs to subdivide a particular organization into smaller communities. When we realized, however, that these subgroups have a shared purpose and they depend on each other to learn and grow, we concluded they were critical to any program for executing strategy. In the past, we would've just labeled this as teamwork, which it certainly is. But we believe it is also a form of community learning that needs to be intentionally nurtured.

An organization's leadership team is the small group of senior leaders who are ultimately responsible for the overall direction of the company. In the repeatable methodology described in Chapter 7, this group makes the critical choices that determine strategy, including mission, values, strategic position, vision, and the goals statement. This group holds itself accountable for how well plans are developed and executed. It has the longest learning loop in the company. In other words, feedback on some of its decisions may take several quarters or even multiple years to understand how well these decisions were made.

This group has to make the tough decisions about how to allocate resources and what things to "stop" doing to free up resources to be used for executing their strategy. The group's decisions, leadership, and management skills have a huge impact on the success of the organization. Part of the coach's role is to figure out how to better support and develop the company's leadership team.

The Initiative Team Community

Early in our fieldwork, we didn't give nearly enough attention to the importance of initiatives and the teams that lead them. We were trying to have the leadership team community solve too many of the problems and build too many of the plans. This resulted in a shortage of the engagement necessary at the mid and lower levels of the organization. We began to realize a "community" existed at the middle layer of organizations, a community with a special set of interests and characteristics that were different than those of the senior layer. Groups at this level are called *initiative teams.*

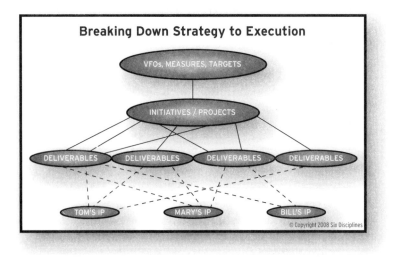

Figure 10.1–How strategy breaks down into executable initiatives, projects, deliverables and individual plans

An initiative (Figure 10.1) is another name for the detailed plan that is followed to accomplish some outcomes or goals. There are two types of such plans: one is known as a corporate initiative and the other a departmental plan (or initiative). The corporate initiative is similar to a project. It has an end, and it's designed to bring about some change in the capability of the organization. A departmental initiative, in contrast, is a plan for a particular department. It usually lasts for a year and has a very different purpose, namely, to organize the ongoing priorities of the department or to address smaller projects that aren't considered corporate initiatives. You can think of a departmental initiative as an annual plan for the department.

Employees who work on initiatives in general are a community because they have a shared set of characteristics and interests that are different than the leadership team. These initiative workers need to understand the company strategy and connect that strategy with the details of how work gets done in the company. For example, what are the processes for generating leads, building products, or delivering services? They have to learn how to build operating plans, sequence work, allocate resources, and integrate the different domains of expertise such as sales or engineering, just as the senior leadership team has to work together to learn from their strategy and planning errors.

Initiative teams have to learn from the experience of multiple projects how to do this effectively. In this sense, they are a different kind of community with a different purpose than the senior leadership team. Senior leadership depends on the initiative team to translate strategy into action plans and to set realistic expectations of what can be done, when, and with how much resource.

The Departmental Team Community

In most organizations, departments are formed around a particular area of expertise, such sales, marketing, services, engineering, manufacturing, purchasing, accounting, or human resources. Corporate initiatives do not account for all the planning that needs to happen in order to run the business. Corporate initiatives are focused on a few strategic changes in the capability of the organization. Each department, however, needs specific plans that support the various sustaining activities of the company including employee training, routine process improvements, and allocation of resource to on-going measure-driven activities (e.g., sales prospecting and customer service calls.)

Department groups are different than initiative communities because they typically share a common area of expertise. Organizations depend on departments to develop deep expertise in their area of responsibility. Sales and marketing departments need to learn how to generate and qualify leads, and close them; engineering teams need to learn how to translate customer input and market requirements into designs. The strength of these communities and how well they do their jobs determine the strength of the initiative teams, since all initiative participants come from one or more departmental teams.

The Team Leader-Team Member Community

The team leader-team member community is by far the smallest of organizational communities. Eventually all work is performed at the individual level, but in concert with others. The team leader-team member relationship serves as the foundation for a strong organization. The relationship of this smallest group in the company is analogous to families and countries. Just as the strength of a nation is rooted in the strength of its families, the strength of an organization depends on the strength of the relationship between team leader and team member.

This community shares a common interest in maximizing the performance and potential of individuals as part of its contribution to company goals. Because this community is small, it encourages the open dialogue necessary to understand an individual's personal and professional goals. Like all communities, this one is based on mutual trust and respect. And because it's a one-on-one relationship, it can share hopes, dreams and challenges that may not be adequately addressed elsewhere.

The strategy execution program described in this book depends on the individual developing self-managing and self-leadership skills. It demands that individuals grow in their ability to understand company strategy, how they fit into it, and to take responsibility and accountability for planning and executing their part of the plan. It's all about *learning how* to do these things.

In this relationship, the team leader mentors, encourages and holds the individual accountable. As with all communities, this community shares the desire for both the individual and the company to reach their potential.

The Company Community

The smaller teams just described are, of course, a part of the larger company community. The company community shares the mission, values, strategic position, and vision. Sharing a common purpose helps people stay engaged and contribute more. We're designed as social creatures, endowed with amazing creative abilities, and a desire for good stewardship of our relationships and opportunities. But since none of us is equipped with identical skills and abilities, we can't achieve our maximum potential unless we join together with others and learn to function as one. Achievement of this potential requires lifelong learning both as an individual and as a community.

The complete program for the pursuit of excellence that we are describing depends on building a sense of common purpose and the realization that this pursuit is a journey. And because it's a journey rather than a destination, it requires an enduring approach. One of the key roles of leadership is to build and protect this vital community. This requires time, energy, and a repeatable approach that nurtures the learning process.

Cross-Company Roles Community

Another community, one external to the company, whose emergence we anticipate consists of individuals sharing with others in the same roles in other companies. This isn't a new idea. For CEOs, groups such as Vistage International, TAB (The Alternative Board), and online CEO groups such as PeerSightOnline.com use a peer-CEO coaching framework. The participants are essentially CEOs helping other CEOs. The establishment of a complete strategy execution program opens the door for accelerated learning among such groups because they share a common purpose, a common set of terminology, and a common approach to pursue that purpose.

The Internet's Impact on Community Formation

Chapter 5 was devoted to the question why now? The Internet, along with the collaborative tools created in the last fifteen years, has transformed our ability to economically establish communities. It has created a compounding force that can overcome the significant barriers in the Execution Revolution for small and midsized businesses.

Internet-based knowledge sharing tools such as forums, wikis, blogs, and instant messaging, as well as online collaboration and communication techniques like RSS feeds, podcasts and tagging, are as revolutionary as they are elegant. They're simple to use and allow almost real-time communication to occur within the communities they serve. They seem to engage workers at an intuitive level, collecting implicit knowledge in natural, accessible ways, and enabling the transfer of that knowledge quickly and efficiently.

Thanks to technology advances, and especially to the involvement by younger generations of workers, a growing number of organizations are using collaborative and social networking tools like wikis, blogs, forums and instant messaging. These tools are improving performance and fostering improved knowledge transfer through innovation and organizational learning.

The power of online communities and the speed with which they have formed is staggering:

- The online auction leader eBay has grown from 2.2 million registered users in 1999 to 181 million registered users in 2005. In September 2007, eBay reported that merchandise worth $12.6 billion was sold *in one quarter*, a 17-percent increase over the previous year. It's likely eBay will exceed $50 billion in 2008.

- Amazon attracts 50 million customers (many repeat) in the U.S. alone every month.
- Google, the global Internet search leader, serves more than 59 million unique visitors each month, performing more than 200 million searches per day.

The Importance of Learning

Now that we appreciate the impact and power of communities, let's shift our focus to the *learning* side of community learning. To do this, we must understand the nature of learning, and, in particular, the nature of adult learning within organizations. When people are all learning, the communities grow stronger. The adult learning scenario is not without its challenges, however.

Perhaps the most critical organizational challenge is assuming that every employee has the desire to learn. According to Dan Bobinski, CEO and Director of The Center for Workplace Excellence, "it can be considered socially unacceptable for a manager or a seasoned professional to demonstrate the desire to learn. For example, because new managers must acquire a whole new skill set, attending management training, in some circles, can be viewed as a weakness."

In this scenario, a big barrier to fostering a community of adult learning can be pride. The only way to remove that barrier is for those at the top of the organization to set the example. If senior leadership openly displays a passion for learning (in this case, a new way of learning to execute strategy effectively) and praises those around them who also seek to learn, then a learning community is likely to accelerate.

What Is Being Shared?

So far, we're seeing many types of information being shared among the communities described earlier. We're certain that what is being shared today will be significantly deeper and richer five years from now.

Following is just a partial list of the kinds of strategy execution program learning that has already started to emerge, or is likely to emerge as these communities grow:

- **Peer group sharing**—meetings between CEO's to share discoveries and experiences
- **Project management**—teams are learning to set clear objectives and sharing techniques for keeping the team on schedule
- **Team member development**—all team members having quarterly self-ratings allows the whole organization to identify weaknesses and best practice opportunities
- **Benchmarks**—for businesses in the same industry, certain benchmark measures that can be shared by the whole community (Our first examples are related to practicing the methodology itself, such as percent of deliverables completed as planned, or the reasons for missed deliverables)

- **Business document templates**—templates for commonly used documents such as stakeholder surveys, corporate plan documents, initiative plans, and individual plans
- **Mainstream processes**—templates that incorporate best practices for many common business practices: hiring and appraising personnel, managing projects, marketing, sales, innovation management, recognition management, complaint management, project work breakdown structures, and so on
- **Gradecards and measures**—performance assessment tools optimized for particular departments or functions
- **Training**—video and audio instructional clips by the community members themselves sharing what is and what is not working in the field
- **Implementation checklists**—tools to assist preparing for annual planning, conducting planning retreats, quarterly reviews, initiative workshops, IP workshops, gradecard workshops, process workshops

[SUMMARY]

- The Execution Revolution will be built around communities with the following characteristics:
  - A belief that their ultimate core competence is the ability to execute their strategy
  - A shared repeatable methodology that organizes their efforts to execute better

- Accountability coaches who are experts in the repeatable methodology they share
- Shared technology (an execution system) to help integrate planning and activity alignment at all levels of the organization
- Active communities in the Execution Revolution consist of communities with these titles: coaches, leadership teams, initiative teams, team leader and team members, and cross-company roles.
- Among adult learners, the biggest barrier to fostering a learning community is pride. For senior leadership, the only way to remove this barrier is to display a passion for learning how to execute strategy effectively.

Of all the four components of a complete program—a repeatable methodology, accountability coaching, an execution system, and a learning community—learning community has the most transforming power. The other three components are prerequisites to leveraging the community. In this regard, learning community has the potential to be the most transforming component of all.

The Execution Revolution starts inside organizations that are passionate about learning and about transforming their capabilities to execute. As more small and midsized businesses participate in this Execution Revolution, the cumulative effect is a growing community that has as much potential to transform how organizations execute strategy as eBay has had transforming auctions, Amazon has had transforming book sales, and Google has had transforming searches and advertising. Also consider the powerful impact the following communities are having by accelerating organizational learning:

- BNI (transforming business networking and business referrals)
- Chambers of Commerce (transforming business development and community investment)
- Vistage and Young Presidents Organizations (transforming the way CEOs can share, network, and learn best practices)
- Economic Development Councils (transforming the way communities encourage business growth)

It's early, and the Execution Revolution is still in its infancy, but the compounding of early successes and transformations will lead to more organizations adopting a new, more effective way of executing strategy.

Now that you have an overview of what a complete strategy execution program requires, the next chapter will focus on what benefits you can derive from adopting and embracing such a program.

CHAPTER 11

[Make Solving All
Other Problems Easier]

> **"** A growing organization, while an exciting ride, is absolutely the most difficult circumstance under which to execute strategy.**"**

Now that you have an overview of what a complete strategy execution program consists of, let's take a deeper look at its benefits. Before we do, however, let's recap the main ideas we've discussed in earlier chapters.

- Every business regularly faces new, often large challenges that it has no control over. Among these are competitors, the economy, the weather, government regulations, and technology. And whatever their challenges are today, they will be different tomorrow.

- All organizations, large and small, struggle to execute strategy *and* deal with unexpected challenges. It's similar to fighting a war on two fronts. *This* is the biggest problem in business.

- Large businesses continue to piece together many *separate* best practices, such as strategic planning, quality management, ERP, knowledge management, and performance management, to help fight this war.

- Such best practices, in combination with the Internet, have become the foundation for a complete strategy execution program. For SMBs, a strategy execution program provides a leapfrog opportunity to go from almost no tools at all to a next-generation approach, skipping the current impractical and unaffordable approaches typically used by larger businesses.

- Although building an organization capable of executing its strategy is not easy (nor ever finished), it's one of the few things that an organization *can* control. Executing strategy requires commitment, discipline and investment. It also requires an enduring approach.

- Building and maintaining an aggressive *execution-capable* organization pays off by making it *easier* (not easy) to handle the many unknown problems and challenges that a company will face in the future.

In this chapter, we'll detail the "how" of this last point: *how* having an organization that knows how to execute strategy makes solving all other problems *easier.*

Managing Growth

An organization that's not growing is much easier to manage than one that is growing. This isn't hard to understand when you realize that most of us become good at doing something by doing it over and over until we master it. An organization that's not growing creates an environment where very little changes. The workforce eventually learns how to make everything work together by the process of simple repetition.

A growing organization, in contrast, hires more people, and promotes people to positions they've never held before. It installs new systems and technologies, implements new processes, provide new services, adds new customers, and so on. The environment is changing constantly. While an exciting ride, a business that's growing rapidly is absolutely the *most* difficult circumstance under which to execute strategy.

An organization that learns a systematic way of setting its priorities, that learns how to build detailed plans, that learns how to proactively manage those plans and communicate in an organized way is in a much better position. In such an environment, goals are clearer and new employees can understand their role sooner. They learn how to communicate more effectively. Overall, the efficiency and effectiveness of the organization will be higher; it will have better capacity to respond to the demands of growth.

In addition, when growth comes and priorities have to change quickly, the organization already knows how to make decisions, build plans, and deploy and execute these plans. It has a much better chance of performing predictably. The alternative creates a whole host of other problems, for example, overworked employees, quality problems, poorly qualified team leaders, hiring mistakes, and disgruntled or unproductive employees. It doesn't take much growth to push an unprepared organization over the edge—and back into Quadrant III.

To better understand this relationship between speed (growth rate) and execution, we used the Value Line database to analyze the quarterly financial data from 1985 to 2005 of 200 publicly traded companies. The results appear in Figure 11.0, which plots the relationship between how fast company earnings are growing (vertical axis) and how variable these earnings are (horizontal axis). The curved line flowing through the data points shows the general trend. This study demonstrates that on the average, once growth rates exceed about 15 percent, unpredictability increases faster than profitability. It also demonstrates that some companies are much better than others at being predictable, even at the same growth rate.

In Figure 11.0, notice that Company A (the company on the left) is growing at about 18 percent a year. So is Company B (on the right). Company A, however, has a volatility (standard

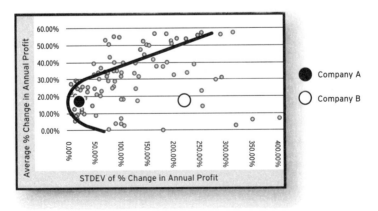

Figure 11.0–The relationship between earnings and variability

deviation) of about 15 percent, while Company B has a volatility of close to 250 percent. Over a period of years they average the same returns, so who cares? The answer is investors care, and so do you. Read on to see why.

The Sleep-at-Night Factor

Not having some sense of what is going to happen in your business next quarter, next month, or even next week is what Six Disciplines' CFO Brian Clark calls the *sleep-at-night* factor.

Figure 11.1 provides a different look at Company A and B. This chart illustrates the *quarterly growth rate in sales* over a five-year period for Company A and B. Even though over a twenty year period they both achieved the same compound earnings growth, which business would you prefer to manage? How would you sleep at night? While I know nothing personally about these two companies, it appears there is something cyclical going on in Company B, but it isn't in the same quarters each year.

The people in that business *may* have total confidence in what's going on, but as an investor or outsider, Company B looks to be pretty nerve-wracking.

My point? An organization that knows how to execute its strategy *and* deal with day-to-day surprises operates in a less stressful environment and, as you will see, increases its value.

Substantially Increase the Value of Your Business

I know I am "preachin' to the choir" when I say that predictable, profitable execution is difficult. A great deal of this book

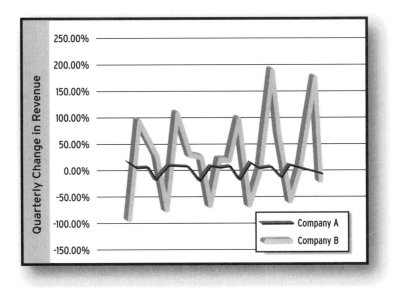

Figure 11.1–The tale of two companies: growth and volatility

is based on this assumption, and I don't find any experienced business leaders who disagree. That's the bad news. The good news is that because it's difficult, it's rare, and because it's rare, it's valuable. A successful business broker made the following statement: "any business that would adopt a systematic program for strategy execution two years before selling the business would get *30–40 percent more* for the business when sold." Why? Because having an organization that knows how to plan and execute is rare. Those who achieve it set themselves apart and are worth more.

This general idea was confirmed in an interesting study conducted in 2005 by the University of Virginia and Rice University analyzing correlations in the price of publicly traded stock.[1] The findings indicated there was a significant correlation between what investors were willing to pay for a stock and its historical sales growth, return on assets, research and development spending, and volatility of cash flow.

Figure 11.2 shows the results of the study. Cash flow volatility had the greatest impact on the price of a stock by almost twice as large a margin as the second, third, and fourth place items. Also notice that this correlation is *negative*. This means that a 100-percent *increase* in a stock's volatility would result in a 37-percent average *reduction* in the value of the stock.

Why is this important to you? Someday, you may want to obtain financing from your bank in order to expand your current business or to buy another business. Someday, you may even want to sell your business or pass it on to someone else. This study suggests that the value of your business will be *significantly* higher if it has a predictable strategy execution history. And on top of all of this, what's it worth to be able to sleep at night?

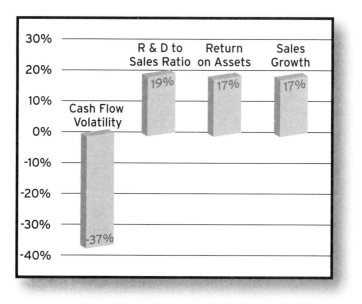

Figure 11.2–Correlation of factors with valuation of a business

[SUMMARY]

- Building an organization that can learn how to execute strategy *and* deal with the daily surprises of the business world is *solving the one problem that makes solving all other problems easier.*

- Solving this one problem yields substantial long-term benefits for your business, including predictability, balance, managed growth, and substantially increased market value. All of this promotes a better night's sleep for you.

- Solving this one problem also leads to the creation of an organization that is *trusted* both internally and externally. It enables an organization that learns how to develop its people to their fullest potential. It empowers an organization that can be successfully transitioned to the next generation, and so on. There's just not enough room in this book to list all of the benefits of pursuing the ongoing journey of strategy execution excellence!

- The value of your business will be significantly higher if it has a predictable strategy execution history.

You now have a better idea of what a complete strategy execution program entails, and just a few of the benefits that are derived from implementing such a program. What you don't have yet is a sense of just how powerful effective strategy execution really is. The final chapter will provide a taste of what can be accomplished when all elements of a complete strategy execution program are working together in harmony.

CHAPTER 12

[An Enduring Pursuit]

" An enduring pursuit requires
an enduring approach.*"*

Among my favorite characters in the Bible are the "men of Issachar." They were advisors to a king, and all that is known about them is that they *"understood the times, and knew what to do about them."* My hope is that I have helped you understand the times, and now know what to do.

The die is cast. Industry progress over the past several decades has made it inevitable that eventually all businesses will have access to and the advantages of some sort of complete strategy execution program—in fact such a program will become a requirement to business survival, just as telephones, computers and the Internet are now. The four core elements of such a program are a repeatable methodology, accountability coaching, an execution system, and community learning. After several years of research and field testing, we now understand how to interweave these four components into a synergistic and complete program. None of the components alone is sufficient. In fact, we don't believe any one of them can be removed without compromising the long-term sustainability of the program. This is why other approaches don't last: they're incomplete.

Although we've described these four elements in terms of our own methodology and coaching model, we know that the core principles of a strategy execution program transcend any one brand. What's clear to us now is that to achieve the kind of results needed and to overcome the barriers identified previously, *all* next-generation approaches will need to incorporate some form of these four elements.

Without experiencing this program firsthand, it's difficult to understand the synergy of the four elements—in other words, to experience the truth that sometimes one plus one does equal three. All four elements *together* provide the breadth and depth of expertise required at an economic price point that works for small and midsized businesses. All four of them *together* help overcome the natural tendency in all of us to let the urgent overcome the important. In our experience, any approach that doesn't address this fact of human nature is unsustainable. It may work for a while, but it will eventually fade away and go the way of most good intentions—just like a fad diet.

To help you think more clearly about the fundamental principles at work in this program, I want to share an area of study that has illuminated many business and life principles for me. This may appear to be a detour from our primary topic and way out of context. But the truths I'm about to explain have become part of my personal fabric, and they're inextricably integrated into the concepts behind the program that drives the Execution Revolution.

The Power of Compounding

I began studying the fascinating topic of compound interest about twenty years ago, and I continue to be fascinated by it today. The more I study compounding, the more I see that it illustrates fundamental principles that guide the pursuit of excellence in all areas of life. Early in my research into the topic, I came across the following quote by Albert Einstein: "... *compound interest is the greatest mathematical discovery of all time.*" This, from a man who spent his entire life exploring the secrets of the cosmos and how creation functions! Why would someone who understood scientific truths that go beyond what most of us can't even imagine be so intrigued by compound interest?

Compound interest is a simple idea that can be summarized as getting interest on your interest. As an example, if I deposit $100 today in an account that yields 5 percent interest, one year from now I will have $100 plus $5 interest, or $105. After two years I will have $105 plus $5.25 interest, or $110.25, and so on. Compound interest is really just a simpler example of geometric growth that we see in nature all the time. A baby is conceived as one cell that splits into two, and the two cells split into four, and so on.

The popular book *Six Degrees of Separation* illustrates a similar concept: I have ten friends, each of whom has ten other friends, each of whom has ten friends. And after six levels, everyone knows everyone in the world.[1] An often-told parable in statistics and investment classes illustrates how few people really understand this principle, and the advantage to those who act on it:

Back in ancient Persia, a king ruled over a large kingdom with great riches and power, but he was bored. So his grand vizier (advisor) invented a game for the king that today we know as chess. The vizier showed the king his newly minted strategy game and the king was delighted with the diversion. And the king was so grateful that he told the vizier to name his reward for the great invention.

The wise old vizier knew exactly what he wanted. He humbly asked the king to place one grain of wheat on the first square of the chessboard, two grains on the second square, four grains on the third, eight grains on the fourth, and so on, doubling the pile in each consecutive square until all 64 squares of the chessboard had doubled the preceding pile of wheat. This was all that the vizier wanted as his reward. The king was amazed at his small request, as the huge royal granaries were brimming with wheat from the year's bountiful harvest. The king offered a more desirable prize such as gold, precious gems, or even a palace. But the grand vizier refused the king's generosity and stuck to his request for the piles of wheat on the chessboard squares.

The king finally shook his head in disbelief and consented to the vizier's strange reward. He summoned his granary manager to begin placing the piles of wheat on the chessboard squares. Initially, the piles of wheat were very small. After the first row of eight squares, only 255 total grains of wheat had been piled on the chessboard, hardly a handful of wheat. Yet, as the granary workers continued to haul in and count out the grains, the piles grew larger and larger. Soon they filled the whole room even though the chessboard still had most of its squares waiting for wheat. Finally the king realized that he had been tricked by his shrewd old vizier, and that all the granaries in his kingdom couldn't meet his pledge.

The king became the victim of the power of compounding. Einstein understood it, the vizier understood it, but do we?

To further illustrate my point, the table in Figure 12.0 can be built in a few short minutes using the Future Value function of a spreadsheet. I'll use this table to illustrate some of the key principles that are important in the pursuit of excellence.

When teaching these principles to young people, I ask them if they could save three dollars a day from age twenty all the way to eighty, given that 80 is the life expectancy of

The Power of Compounding

	Baseline	Minus $1	Plus $1	CD Rate	Delay 1-Day	Delay 1-Wk	Delay 1-Mo	Delay 1-Yr	Delay 5-yrs	Improve 10%
Amount	$3	$2	$4	$3	$3	$3	$3	$3	$3	3.3
Interest	11%	11%	11%	5%	11%	11%	11%	11%	11%	12%
Number of Days	21,900	21,900	21,900	21,900	21,899	21,893	21,870	21,535	20,075	24,090
Result ($0)	$7,300	$4,867	$9,734	$418	$7,298	$7,285	$7,235	$6,539	$4,208	$29,213
Difference ($0)		($2,433)	$2,433	($6,882)	($2)	($15)	($66)	($761)	($3,092)	$21,913

© Copyright 2008 Six Disciplines

Figure 12.0–An example of future value, and the power of compounding

an average male adult in the U.S. Most say, yes, this wouldn't be too difficult. Next, I ask how much money they think they would have at the end of that time if they invested it in the stock market. Few even know where to start, so I suggest that they simply round it off to $1,000 a year ($3 x 365 = $1,095) and multiply by sixty years. That comes to $60,000 principle invested. Once this is known, you can estimate the interest (rate of return) on the money that had been saved over that period of time.

The answer to this simple example is in column 2, labeled "Baseline." Three dollars a day, compounded daily at a rate of return of 11 percent for sixty years (21,900 days) would produce a sum of $7.3 million!

Just as in the chessboard and wheat example, this is a shocking result. If you invest only $60,000 for sixty years, how can it possibly turn into $7.3 million? Over the years, I've found that shocking results (whether good or bad) are an invitation to learn something, perhaps something big. In the interest of brevity, I'm going to list just a few of the lessons I've learned as a result.

How Much Are You Willing To Invest?

The first parameter in row 1 of Figure 12.0 represents the decision to invest three dollars a day. What if you decide to invest two dollars a day instead? This modest change results in $2.4 million *less* at the end of the period (column 2). If you invest four dollars a day, it results in a total of $9.7 million or an increase of $2.4 million. What's the fundamental principle behind this? It's not about money. Money is a fairly recent invention that represents the fruit of our labors—our time and energy and skill. It's a way to store the fruit of our labor and exchange it for the fruit of someone else's labor. My point is simply this: we only have so much time and energy. Compound interest instructs us to think carefully about where we invest our time—and how much we invest. This issue is particularly relevant when considering whether to implement a program that will transform the ability of your organization to execute more predictably. How much are you willing to invest?

How Well Do You Manage Risk?

Column 4 of Figure 12.0, labeled "CD Rate," shows what happens if you invest these funds in a certificate of deposit (CD), which is considered to be a safe investment. On average, CDs typically return around 5 percent over long periods of time. The CD has low volatility; it won't go up and down like the stock market. The government and banks provide some level of guarantees on such deposits. A CD can turn the investment of $60,000 into $418,000. However, that's $6.9 million less than our primary example. In this case, the price of *safety* is pretty high.

Return on investment and risk are related. Rate of return in the financial world is a function of how well risks are managed. At the principle level, I believe the compound interest model teaches us that the first decision we make is how much of ourselves are we going to invest in a particular pursuit. The second decision related to return is really about the wisdom to manage risk. How well do we understand what is going on around us, and how skilled are we in making decisions? Wisdom is about balancing and controlling risks. This is a much deeper principle than just finance. It applies to recreation, relationships, vocational choices, and every other area of our lives. The purpose of a strategy execution program is to provide a systematic way for the organization to learn how to make and execute better decisions: in other words, to stay in Quadrant II longer.

The Price of Delay

The "Delay 1" columns illustrate how costly it is to delay acting. A delay of one day (three dollar) reduces the eventual outcome by $2,000 dollars. It's not intuitive that the price of the delay is determined at the *end* of the period rather than the *beginning*. A delay of one week costs $15,000. A one-month delay costs $66,000. A one year delay costs $761,000. Five years costs $3.1 million. So what's the more fundamental principle that transcends finance? The failure to act on the truth that we know is expensive. In fact, the results can never be recovered. Notice that *not* acting when you don't know the direction is not delay. The kind of delay we're speaking of is knowing what to do, but *not* doing it. Whether it's improving your hiring process, long-term planning, or some sort of accountability program—nothing happens until you start!

Sticking With It

The principle of sticking with it is best illustrated by Figure 12.1. This graph show what happens in the baseline case in terms of the increase in value over a sixty-year period. Several truths are contained in this diagram. First is the value of both patience and endurance. It takes incredible focus and faith in what you're doing to have the confidence that it will pay off. Notice, in this figure, how it appears that almost nothing is happening during the first thirty years. Now, however, notice that the value of the investment almost triples in the last ten years. It takes a great deal of faith, courage, and experience to know what is and is not right, and stay the course when everything within you is shouting to do something else. When it comes to building an excellent business, many times it will seem like nothing is happening.

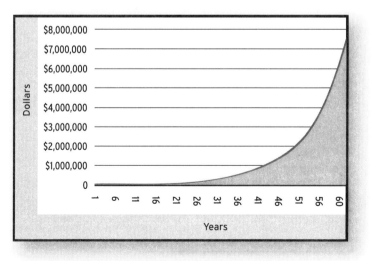

Figure 12.1–Plotting the increase in baseline value over time

The Little Things Count

This is probably the most hidden truth of all. Remember that the only differences between the $7.3 million and the $60,000 dollars invested was compounding of interest. In this example, we were calculating interest and compounding it daily. To really understand this principle fully, let's do that.

The interest on one day's deposit is $0.0009, or nine hundredths of one cent ($3 x 11% annual rate / 365 days in a year). Think about this for a moment. The difference of compounding this tiny fraction of a penny *is* the difference between having your $60,000 turn into $7.3 million.

The broader principle and application is that *the little things in life matter*. It also means that doing the little things right for a long period of time has unfathomable power. It takes effort, wisdom, and perseverance. A lot of people understand this with their head, but not with their heart. This illustration stirs and challenges me every time I think about it. Building an organization that knows how to execute is based on how you do the little things: every goal you set, every interaction with a team member, every person you hire, every customer interaction. They all matter. And they are all compounding for good or for something else.

The Best is Still Ahead

The next principle, the best is still ahead, is best depicted in Figure 12.2. I gave a keynote speech at a university graduation a few years ago to about 3,000 people. During this speech, I handed out copies of Figure 12.2 and put an arrow on the number 50. As I explained this to them, I pointed out that the principle of

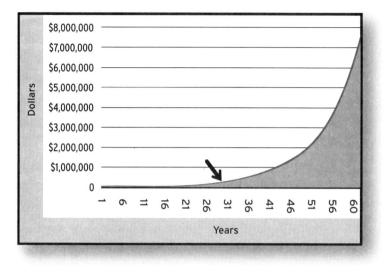

Figure 12.2–The best is still ahead

compounding teaches us our lives are built on our past. Every experience and every relationship all become part of what we can compound into the future as long as we keep going.

The arrow represented me. I was at the point where I was fifty years old—roughly halfway through the sixty-year period of my *adult* life (note that year 1 on the chart starts when I am twenty). I had sold a successful company and could have done almost anything with my life. This graph helped me think carefully about how to build on my past, to not throw away what I already knew but to compound it. Today, my goal is to do this for the rest of my life. And this diagram tells us (you and me) something else, too. For every one of us who practices these truths, the best is still ahead! My body may be creaking a little, but my energy, enthusiasm, and sense of purpose has never been higher. And, fortunately, I'm surrounded by like-minded colleagues and a younger generation (or even two) that are way ahead of me in their respective points on their curve.

Synergy at Work

Synergy is a word that is used heavily in the business world. It refers to multiple components working together to produce more than any one of them could by itself. The last column in Figure 12.0, "Improve 10%," illustrates synergy at work in the world of compounding.

For example, if you were to invest in the "benchmark" program (first column) and improve each of the three factors ($3, 11 percent and 60 years) by 10 percent, how much would the overall output improve? The result is amazing: $7.3 million turns into a whopping $29 million. Ten percent extra produces a 400-percent gain.

What's the broader principle? I believe the message is that the real power in our lives comes from the inside out, our hunger for truth, the wisdom to understand where we're going or what we're doing, how much risk we're willing to take, our commitment to act, and the trust we have in our direction.

Somehow, all of these things work together, in a synergistic way, to produce meaningful fruit that is beyond even what we can hope and dream. The Execution Revolution is based on the principle of synergy. None of the pieces alone will produce the result of all of them combined. This is why individual best practices alone have not been a complete answer to strategy execution problems. Consulting by itself, coaching by itself, software by itself, books, frameworks, methodologies—none of them by themselves will produce even a fraction of the potential.

[SUMMARY]

This chapter is not about finance. It's about life. Following are questions you must ask yourself if you want to live wisely:

- How much of yourself are you willing to invest, and what are you willing to invest in?
- How much risk are you willing to take, and how do you manage it?
- When are you going to start? What is the price of delay?
- How much staying power do you have? How long can you stick with it?
- Do you understand the truth that in compounding the best is ahead, always?
- Do you see the whole: how all the pieces fit together to make a sum greater than the parts?

So what does this all mean as far as the Execution Revolution is concerned? The last chapter contains a few parting thoughts.

Final Thoughts

Recall that this book is based on three core premises. The first premise is that most business leaders are focused on solving the wrong problem. Premise two states that if you focus on solving the right problem, the solution to all other problems will be *easier* (not easy). The last premise is that occasionally in life, all the pieces fall together, creating a leapfrog opportunity to solve old problems.

The Execution Revolution is about a next-generation approach to building organizations that learn to execute strategy in a fundamentally new way. This is an enduring and difficult pursuit that takes an enduring and holistic approach. To achieve the amazing power of synergy discussed in the last chapter, the approach must be complete. If you leave out any of the components, you'll not realize anywhere near the same result.

The program described in this book challenges organizations to consider what they're willing to invest in, and how much they're willing to invest. It teaches organizations how to communicate with each other so they can evaluate and manage risk better, especially when the inevitable surprises occur. The program shows how to become proactive in managing problems and how to minimize the hidden costs of procrastination and delay. It's designed to continually encourage you and your team to *stick with it*, to keep doing what you know you should, when all other circumstances try to distract you. Finally, this complete program is optimized to build organizations that remain focused from top to bottom on long-term goals and strategy. For disciplined, innovative businesses that have an engaged workforce, the best is ahead. Always!

- Take the Execution Revolution Challenge!
  www.SixDisciplines.com/Challenge
- Sign up for our newsletter
  www.SixDisciplines.com/Newsletter
- View client videos, case studies, testimonials
  www.SixDisciplines.com/Clients
- Download forms from the first book (Six Disciplines for Excellence) www.SixDisciplines.com/Forms
- Browse the Six Disciplines Be Excellent blog
  www.SixDisciplines.com/Blog
- Find out more about the author
  www.GaryHarpst.com

Notes

Introduction

1. Solomon Software combined with Great Plains Software
    in 2000. Nine months later, the combined company was
    purchased by Microsoft. The Solomon products are still sold
    today by Microsoft under the Dynamics SL brand name.

Chapter 1

1. Michael Porter, "What is Strategy?" *Harvard Business
    Review,* 1996

2. Download the Sharn Veterinary client case study, as
    well as other Six Disciplines case studies and videos at
    www.SixDisciplines.com.

Chapter 2

1. This story is not original with me. I heard it two or three
    times in the 1980s. The details differed but the point was
    the same.

2. Janamitra Devan, Matthew B. Klusas, and Timothy W.
    Ruefli, "The Elusive Goal of Corporate Outperformance,"
    The McKinsey Quarterly, April 2007

3. Robert Kaplan and David Norton, *The Strategy-Focused Organization*, Harvard Business School Press, 2001

4   Renaissance Solutions Survey, 1996

5. John Kotter, *Leading Change*, 1996

6. American Management Association and Human Resource Institute survey, as reported by Business Finance Magazine Newsletter, Issue 25, March 29, 2007

7. Ralph Welborn and Vince Kasten, *Get It Done! A Blueprint for Business Execution,* Wiley, 2006

8. "The Small Business Economy," U.S. Small Business Administration, 1998

9. *CEO Challenge 2007: Top 10 Challenges,* The Conference Board, October 2007

Chapter 3

1. C. William Pollard, *The Soul of the Firm*, 1996.

2. Peter M. Senge, *The Fifth Discipline: The Art and Practice of the Learning Organization*, 1990 (page 8)

Chapter 4

1. Congressional Budget Office, 2000

2. "Getting Wise With Solomon," PriceWaterhouse Review—Editors Choice, *PC Magazine*, (Reprinted from *PC Magazine*, January 1985, with permission. Copyright © 1985 Ziff Davis Publishing Holdings Inc. All Rights Reserved)

3. David Norton and Randall Russell, *Best Practices in Managing The Execution of Strategy,* Harvard Business School Publishing Corp, 2004

4. "Demographic Trends Report," Pew Internet & Life, April 26, 2006.

5. Sheila Maher, MA., MBA, and Suzi Pomerantz, MT., MCC, "The Future of Executive Coaching: Analysis From a Market Life Cycle Approach," *International Journal of Coaching in Organizations*, 2003

6. Global Coaching Survey Results, Sherpa Coaching, LLC, 2007

7. *Ivy Business Journal*, September-October 2000

8. Stratford Sherman, Alyssa Freas, "The Wild West of Executive Coaching", *Harvard Business Review*, 2004

Chapter 5

1. Gary Harpst, *Six Disciplines for Excellence*, pages 106–107.[2] John P. Kotter, *Leading Change*, 1996

Chapter 7

1. Marcus Buckingham, "Q12—12 Questions That Matter," The Gallup Organization, 1992–1999

2. Stephen R. Covey, *The 8th Habit: From Effectiveness To Greatness*, Free Press, 2004

Chapter 8

1. Jeff Grimshaw, Gregg Baron, Barry Mike, Neill Edwards "How To Combat a Culture of Excuses and Promote Accountability," *Strategy & Leadership*, Vol. 34, No. 5, 2006

2. International Coaching Federation press release, September 2007

3. *Ivy Business Journal*, September-October 2000

4. Stratford Sherman, Alyssa Freas, "The Wild West of Executive Coaching," *Harvard Business Review*, 2004

Chapter 9

1. Robert B. Grady, *Successful Software Process Improvement*, Prentice Hall PTR, 1997

2. Gloria Marks, "The Science of Interruption," *New York Magazine*, 2007

3. Center for Creative Leadership, "10 Trends," CCL research white paper, 2007

4. Karen Renaud, (University of Glasgow), Judith Ramsay (Paisley University) Mario Hair, http://www.nurs.co.uk/news/articles/cms/1187258330212 694732853_1.htm

5. Dr. Monica Seeley, Mesmo Consultancy, www.mesmo.co.uk

Chapter 10

1. David Norton and Randall Russell, *Best Practices in Managing The Execution of Strategy*, Harvard Business School Publishing Corp, 2004

Chapter 11

1. George Allayannis, Brian Roundtree, James P. Weston, *Earnings volatility, cash flow volatility, and firm value*, University of Virginia, Rice University, December 2005.

Chapter 12

1. John Guare, *Six Degrees of Separation*, Dramatists Play Service Inc. 1995

Resources

The following books and websites are highly recommended, many of which influenced or were referenced in *Six Disciplines® Execution Revolution*:

On Execution

- Larry Bossidy, Ram Charan, Charles Burck, *Execution: The Discipline of Getting Things Done*
- Lawrence G. Hrebiniak, *Making Strategy Work: Leading Effective Execution and Change*
- Laurence Haughton, *It's Not What You Say . . . It's What You Do*
- Nitin Nohria, William Joyce, and Bruce Roberson, *What Really Works*
- Ralph Welborn and Vince Kasten, *Get It Done! A Blueprint for Business Execution*
- Jeffrey Pfeffer and Robert I. Sutton, *The Knowing-Doing Gap: How Smart Companies Turn Knowledge into Action*

- Mark Morgan, Raymond Levitt, William Malek, *Executing Your Strategy: How to Break It Down and Get It Done*
- Stephen M.R. Covey, *The Speed of Trust: The One Thing that Changes Everything*

On Strategy

- Michael Porter, *What Is Strategy?*
- Nikos Mourkogiannis, *Purpose: The Starting Point of Great Companies*
- Michael E. Raynor, *The Strategy Paradox: Why Committing to Success Leads to Failure (And What to Do About It)*
- David Maister, *Strategy And The Fat Smoker: Doing What's Obvious But Not Easy*
- Al Ries and Jack Trout, *Positioning: The Battle for Your Mind*

On Business Excellence

- Jim Collins, *Good To Great: Why Some Companies Make The Leap and Others Don't*
- Jim Collins, *Built To Last*
- Tom Peters, *In Search of Excellence*
- Peter F. Drucker, *The Essential Drucker*

On New Perspectives

- Thomas L. Friedman, *The World Is Flat*
- Chris Anderson, *The Long Tail*
- Patricia Aburdene, *Megatrends 2010*
- Chip Heath, Dan Heath, *Made To Stick*
- Ray Kurzweil, *The Singularity is Near*

On Change, Habits

- John P. Kotter, *Leading Change*
- Alan Deutschman, *Change or Die*
- Jagdish N. Sheth, *The Self-Destructive Habits of Good Companies . . . and how to break them*

On Personal Productivity, Time Management

- Stephen Covey, *7 Habits of Highly Successful People*
- Stephen Covey, Roger Merrill, Rebecca Merrill, *First Things First*
- Stephen Covey, *The 8th Habit*
- David Allen, *Getting Things Done*
- Peter F. Drucker, *The Effective Executive: The Definitive Guide to Getting the Right Things Done*

On Small Business Operations/Entrepreneurship

- Michael Gerber, *The E-Myth Revisited*

On Activity Alignment

- Robert S. Kaplan and David P. Norton, *Alignment: Using the Balanced Scorecard to Create Corporate Synergies*
- Steven Anderson and Robert S. Kaplan, *Time-Driven Activity-Based Costing*

On Measurement

- Robert S. Kaplan and David P. Norton, *The Balanced Scorecard*

On Organizational Learning and Communities

- Peter Senge, *The Fifth Discipline*

- Don Tapscott, *Wikinomics: How Mass Collaboration Changes Everything*
- Chip Conley, *Peak: How Great Companies Get Their Mojo From Maslow*

On Business Coaching

- Dan Coughlin, *Accelerate: 20 Practical Lessons To Boost Business Momentum*
- International Coach Federation www.coachfederation.org/ICF/
- The Foundation of Coaching www.thefoundationofcoaching.org/

Market Research Firms

- Gartner www.gartner.com
- AMR Research www.amrresearch.com
- AMI-Partners www.ami-partners.com
- Ventana Research www.ventanaresearch.com
- Bain & Company www.bain.com

Index

Acknowledgements

To the *Six Disciplines Team*, for
"building ships instead of hewing logs."

To *Thomas D (Skip) Reardon*, for the year of extra
effort required to make a long book short. Your ideas and
experience were essential in making this project successful.

To *Jay Marquart*, for your meticulous
editing and proofing of this project.

To *John Crawford* (the first Six Disciplines "pioneer"),
for having the faith upon which we continue to build.
Karen, Ben and *Jenna* are 'doing you proud.'

To all of the *Six Disciplines franchises, coaches*
and *team members* for sharing in the dream, and
taking the risks to bring it to life. What you are
doing is making a difference in the world!

To *Jack Ridge* and *Vern Strong*,
my partners. Proverbs 3:5,6.

To *Norma Ruth Harpst,*
a magnificent person and my mom.

To *Rhonda*, my soul mate, and to
Jamie, Keri, Anna and *Jordan* our joy!

To the *One* who knows the
'end from the beginning.'
The adventure continues!

About the Author

Gary Harpst is the founder and CEO of Six Disciplines, and is also the author of "*Six Disciplines for Excellence: Building Small Businesses That Learn, Lead and Last,*" which reveals  the specific details of the business-building methodology for small and midsized businesses that want to pursue enduring business excellence.

Harpst founded Six Disciplines in the fall of 2000. Today, Six Disciplines offers the Six Disciplines strategy execution program, the result of thousands of hours of market research, 100 man-years of development and field verification, and more than $20 million of funding.

The Six Disciplines program enables organizations to establish core competency in six critical business disciplines related to strategy, planning, organization, execution, innovation and learning. The Six Disciplines program is offered exclusively through Six Disciplines Centers located in major cities across the U.S.

Harpst received a Bachelors degree in Business Administration with a Computer Science major in 1972, and a Masters degree in Business Administration with a Computer Science specialization in 1976—both from the Ohio State University in Columbus, Ohio.

Following several years working for the Ohio State University and for Marathon Oil in Findlay, Harpst became the co-founder and CEO of Solomon Software, Inc., headquartered in Findlay, Ohio. From 1980 through 2000, Solomon Software grew to more than 400 employees and $60 million in annual revenue. During the two decades, Solomon became one of the industry leaders in its market and sold more than 60,000 installations of the Solomon product in over 400 different industries in more than 100 countries worldwide. Solomon merged with Great Plains Software in 2000, and the combined company was later acquired by Microsoft Corporation in 2001. Today, Solomon is part of the Microsoft Dynamics product line.

In addition, Harpst is active in the community with prior involvement with Junior Achievement, as a past board member of the local YMCA and Liberty Benton High School. Harpst currently serves on the University of Findlay Board and is Elder in the St John Mennonite Church. Harpst has a strong interest in learning to integrate his faith in Jesus Christ in business and all of life.

Harpst was also a finalist in Ernst & Young's Entrepreneur of the Year award in 1999. In 2001, he received an honorary doctorate from the University of Findlay for Business Entrepreneurship. More recently, Harpst received the 2004 Small Business Advocate of the Year Award from the Findlay/Hancock County Chamber of Commerce.

In 2004, Harpst also founded Plumbline Solutions, Inc., (www.plumblinesolutions.com), an 80-person Findlay, Ohio-based software engineering service for Microsoft® Independent Software Vendors.

Harpst is a dynamic and insightful public speaker who challenges and motivates his audiences. His presentations weave together the principles and strategies which are the foundation of the Six Disciplines program, with humor, wisdom, energy, and incisive anecdotes from his many years of business management experience. His work as an author, keynote speaker, television and radio guest, and executive mentor has created nationwide interest in applying the Six Disciplines strategy execution program in organizations that passionately want to pursue enduring business excellence. Visit Six Disciplines at www.SixDisciplines.com.

Ready to Join The Revolution?

To further the ideas described in this book and in his first book *Six Disciplines for Excellence*, Gary Harpst has formed Six Disciplines which shows businesses how to implement these principles through a nationwide network of Six Disciplines Centers. If you are interested in becoming a client or you are interested in owning a Six Disciplines Center franchise we encourage you to visit www.SixDisciplines.com.

- Take the Execution Revolution Challenge!
  www.SixDisciplines.com/Challenge
- Sign up for our newsletter
  www.SixDisciplines.com/Newsletter
- View client videos, case studies, testimonials
  www.SixDisciplines.com/Clients
- Download forms from the first book (Six Disciplines for Excellence) www.SixDisciplines.com/Forms
- Browse the Six Disciplines Be Excellent blog
  www.SixDisciplines.com/Blog
- Find out more about the author
  www.GaryHarpst.com

Start Your Own Execution Revolution!

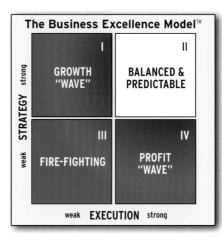

To maintain the necessary balance between strategy and execution, and doing so while overcoming everyday hurdles, requires a complete program consisting of four tightly-integrated components:

- *A Repeatable Methodology* to drive organizational learning and understanding
- *Accountability Coaching* to nurture and nudge you to stay on track
- *An Execution System* to engage everyone, everyday in real-time activity alignment
- *Community Learning* to share and reinforce best practices and to accelerate learning

Take Action Now to Balance Strategy and Execution in Your Organization

- Take the Execution Revolution Challenge!
  www.SixDisciplines.com/Challenge
- Sign up for our newsletter
  www.SixDisciplines.com/Newsletter
- Hear from companies that are balancing strategy and execution with impressive results:
  www.SixDisciplines.com/Clients
- Visit the Be Excellent® blog
  www.SixDisciplines.com/Blog
- Learn more about the author Gary Harpst
  www.GaryHarpst.com
- Find a Six Disciplines Center near you
  www.SixDisciplines.com/Centers
- Order copies (including bulk orders) of
  Six Disciplines® Execution Revolution
  www.SixDisciplinesPublishing.com

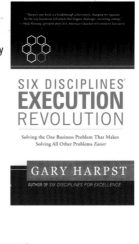